FRANK ZAPPA

AUTHENTIC TRANSCRIPTIONS WITH NOTES AND TABLATURE

- 3 INTRODUCTION
- 8 PEACHES EN REGALIA
- 14 WILLIE THE PIMP
- 30 SON OF MR. GREEN GENES
- 43 LITTLE UMBRELLAS
- 45 THE GUMBO VARIATIONS
- 65 IT MUST BE A CAMEL

Music transcriptions by Andy Aledort

Album cover courtesy of Matt Groening

ISBN 0-634-02152-4

7777 W. BLUEMOUND RD. P.O. BOX 13819 MILWAUKEE, WI 53213

For all works contained herein:
Unauthorized copying, arranging, adapting, recording or public performance is an infringement of copyright.
Infringers are liable under the law.

Zappa, FZ, Frank Zappa, & "The Moustache" are marks belonging to the Zappa Family Trust
Artwork and elements used by permission
All Rights Reserved

Visit Hal Leonard Online at
www.halleonard.com

Anything Zappanese go to
www.zappa.com

When <u>Hot Rats</u> first dropped onto my sick little teenage record player back in 1969, I planted myself on the floor and sandwiched my head between the two speakers, expecting yet another masterpiece from Frank Zappa.

But what another masterpiece!

Even by Frank's brilliant standards, <u>Hot Rats</u> is in a class by itself. With its angular melodies, quick-change rhythms, and eccentric arrangements, <u>Hot Rats</u> basically invented that peculiar musical genre known as fusion. I think it also remains the finest jazz-rock album of all time. Everything about <u>Hot Rats</u>, from Sugarcane Harris's screeching violin to Ian Underwood's exuberant saxes (not to mention Don Van Vliet at his growly Beefheartiest) continues to amaze me. I've been listening to it for more than three decades now, and I keep hearing new things in Frank's extended guitar solos, which play like sneaky little compositions within the bigger pieces. (And does anyone else hear a wee bit of Stravinsky's <u>Petrouchka</u> in "Willie the Pimp"?)

One little confession: the cover of <u>Love Is Hell</u>, my first cartoon book, was inspired by the graphic starkness of the <u>Hot Rats</u> cover. I admitted this to Frank and Gail several years ago, which led to Gail asking me to write this little piece. Gail also asked if I still had my original beat-up LP copy of <u>Hot Rats,</u> so here it is reproduced in all its mottled, stained, dog-eared glory, complete with candle-wax drippings.

HOT RATS . . . HOT ROOTS . . . HOT ZITS . . . what another masterpiece!

                                                               Matt Groening
                                                               Los Angeles
                                                               December 21, 2000

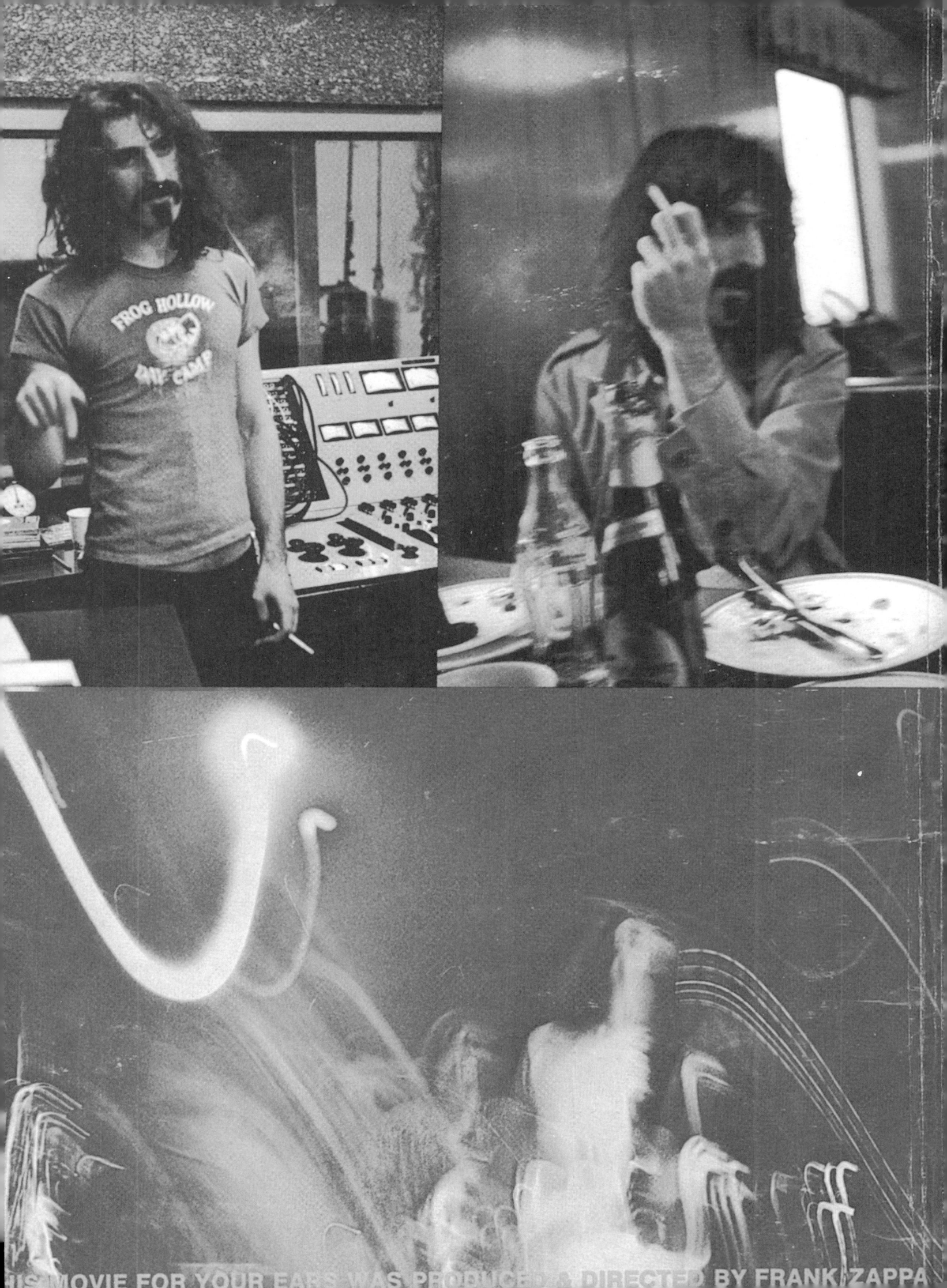

CAPTAIN BEEFHEART

Peaches en Regalia

By Frank Zappa

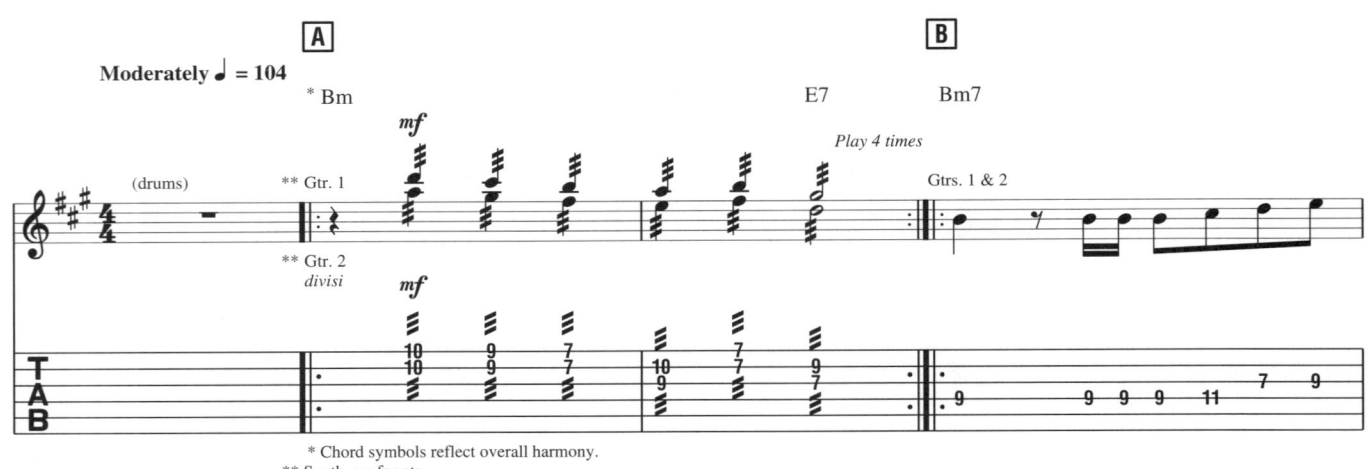

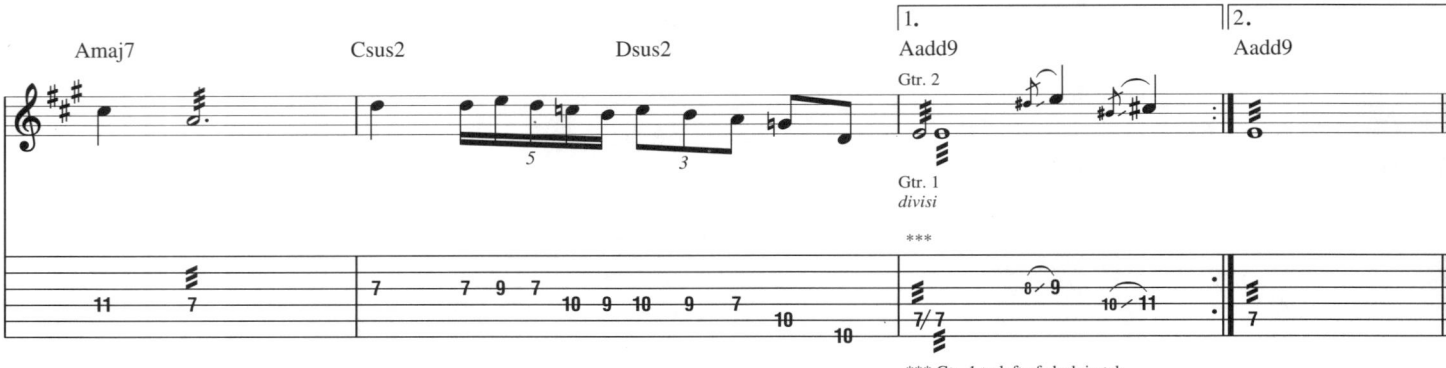

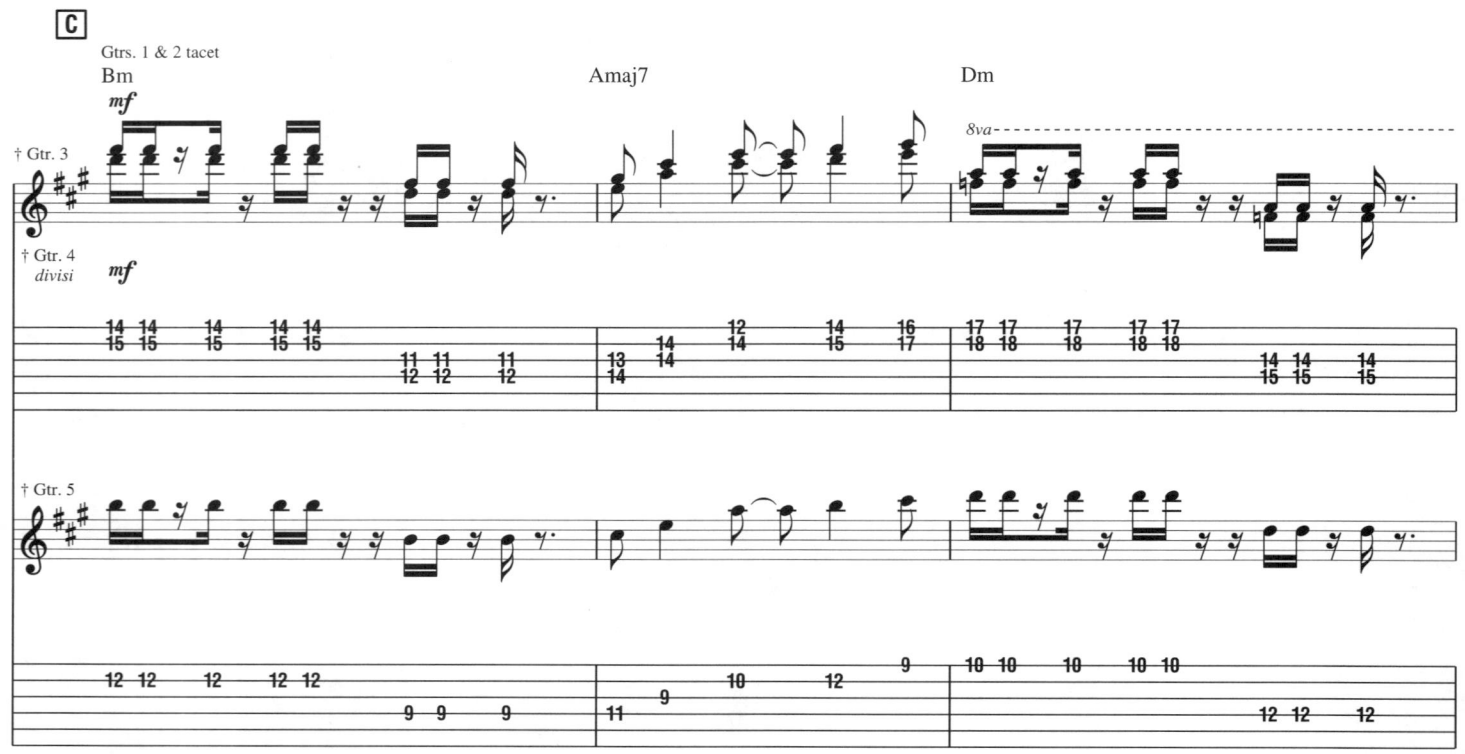

† Sax. arr. for gtr.

All compositions contained herein are © 1969 and controlled worldwide by The Zappa Family Trust
All Rights Reserved   Reprinted by Permission

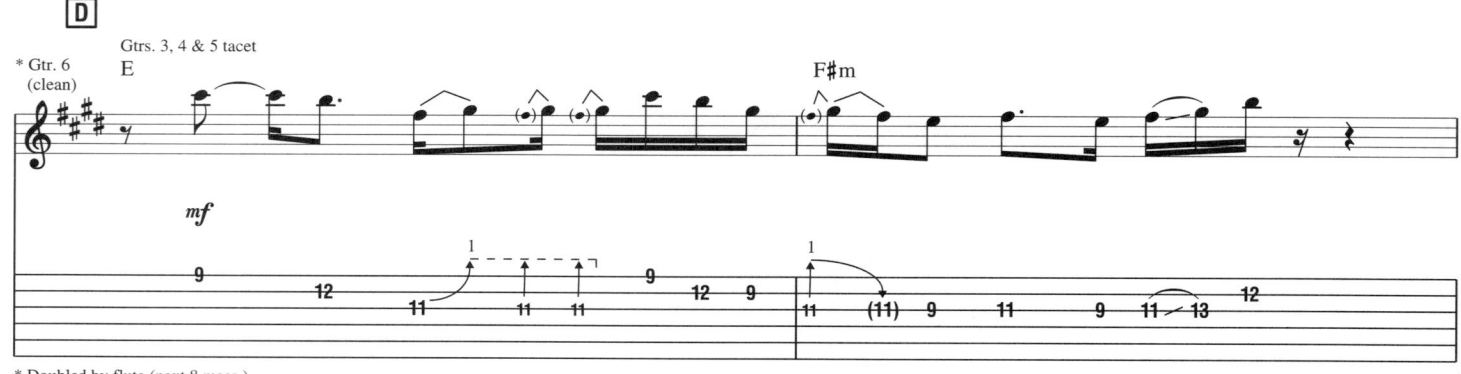
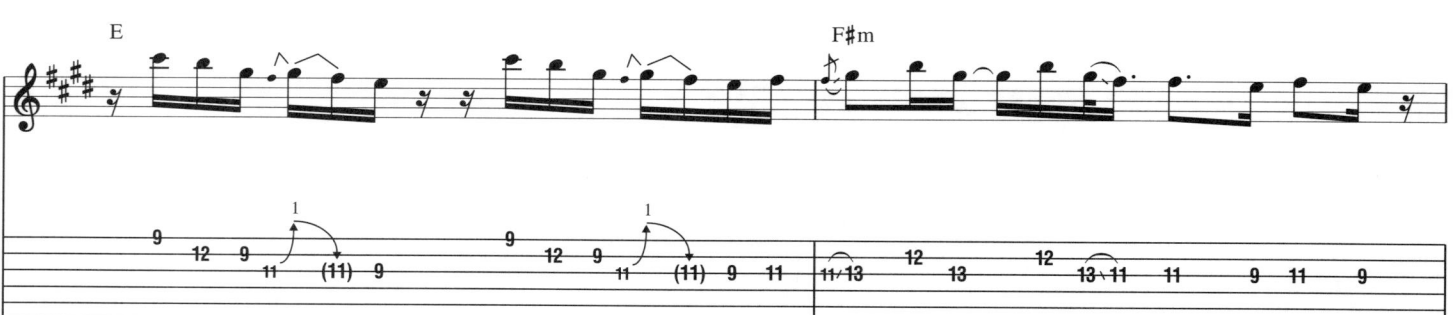
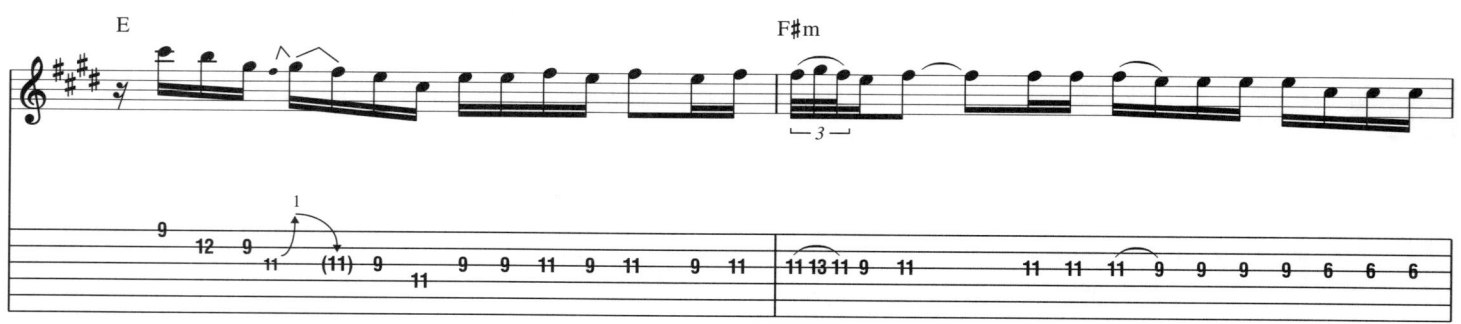
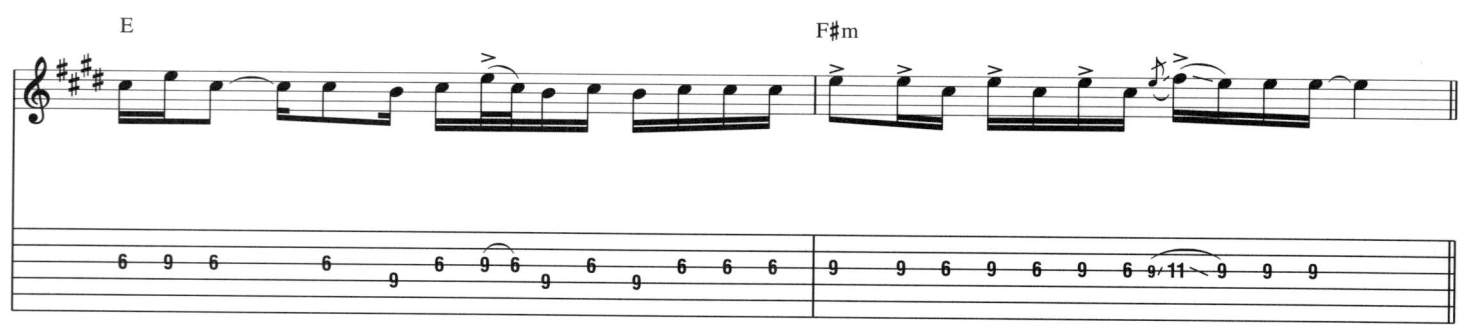
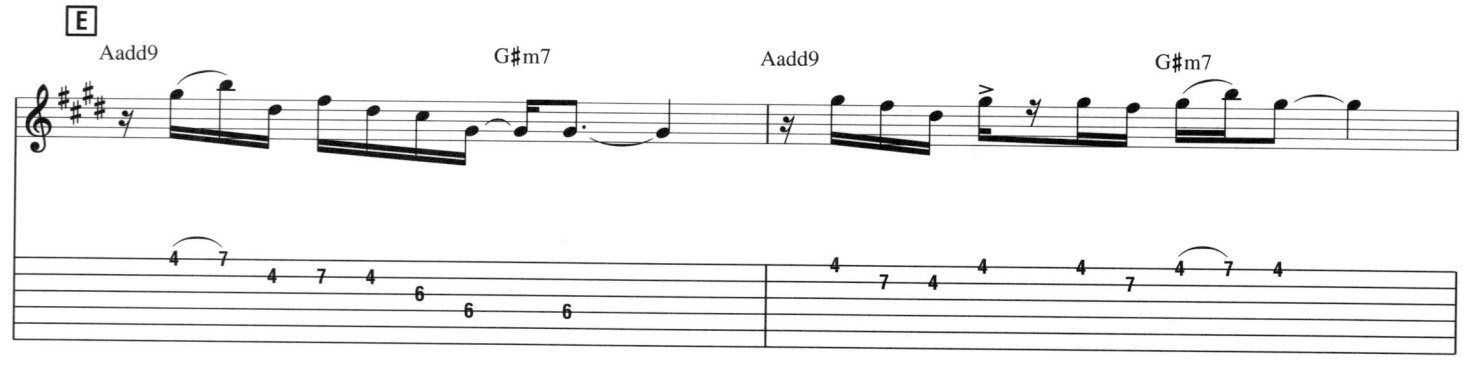

Aadd9
G#m7
Aadd9
G#m7
1/2
1/2
1/2
F
Gtr. 6 tacet
C
D
Bb
Eb
* Gtr. 7
* Organ arr. for gtr.
Ab
F
Gsus2
G7sus4
Gtr. 7
Gtr. 3
Gtr. 4
steady gliss.
Gtr. 5
steady gliss.

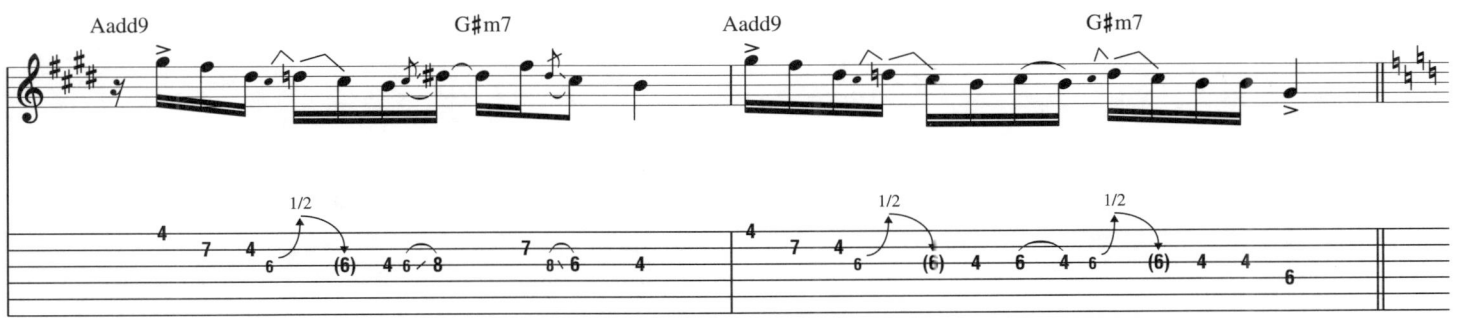

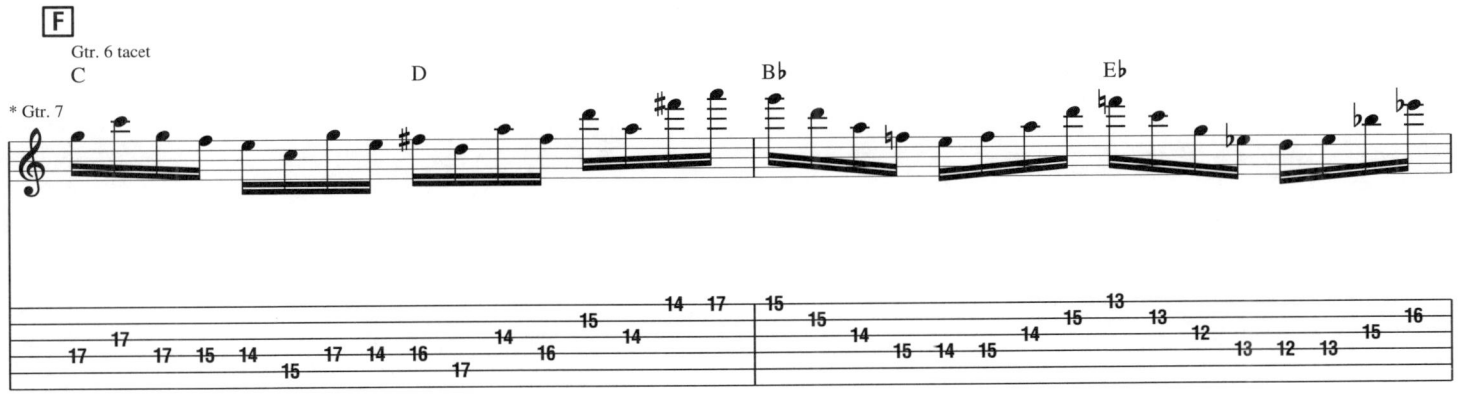

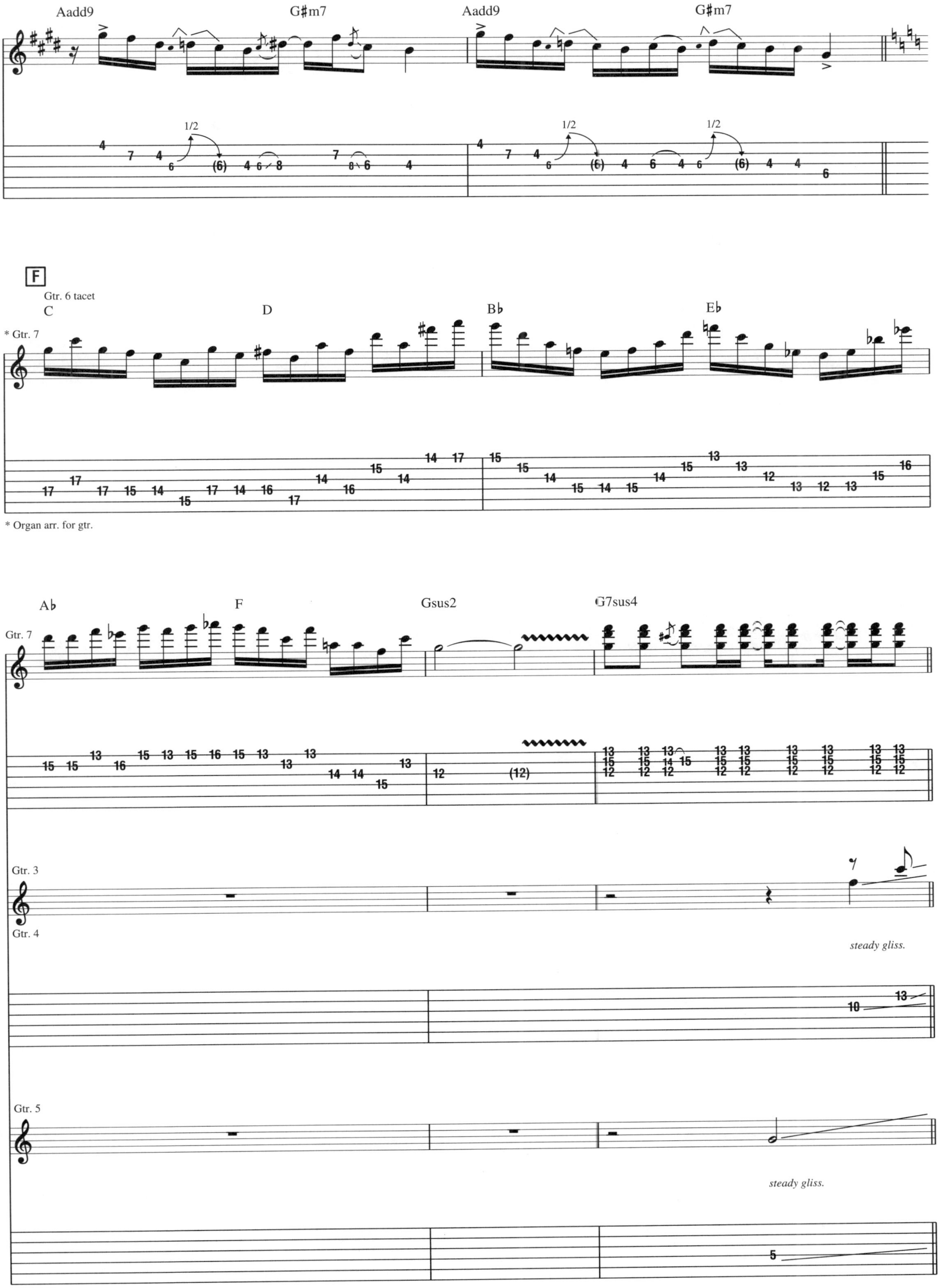

Willie the Pimp

By Frank Zappa

14

neck wan-na buy a grunt with a third par-ty check.
Pre-Chorus
N.C.(Am7)
Stand-in' on-na porch of the Li-co Ho-tel.
Chorus
N.C.(Am)
Flooz-ies in the lob-by love the way I sell hot meat, hot rats, hot
mf
w/ wah-wah/ envelope filter
cash, hot ritz, hot roots, hot soots.
1/4
1/2

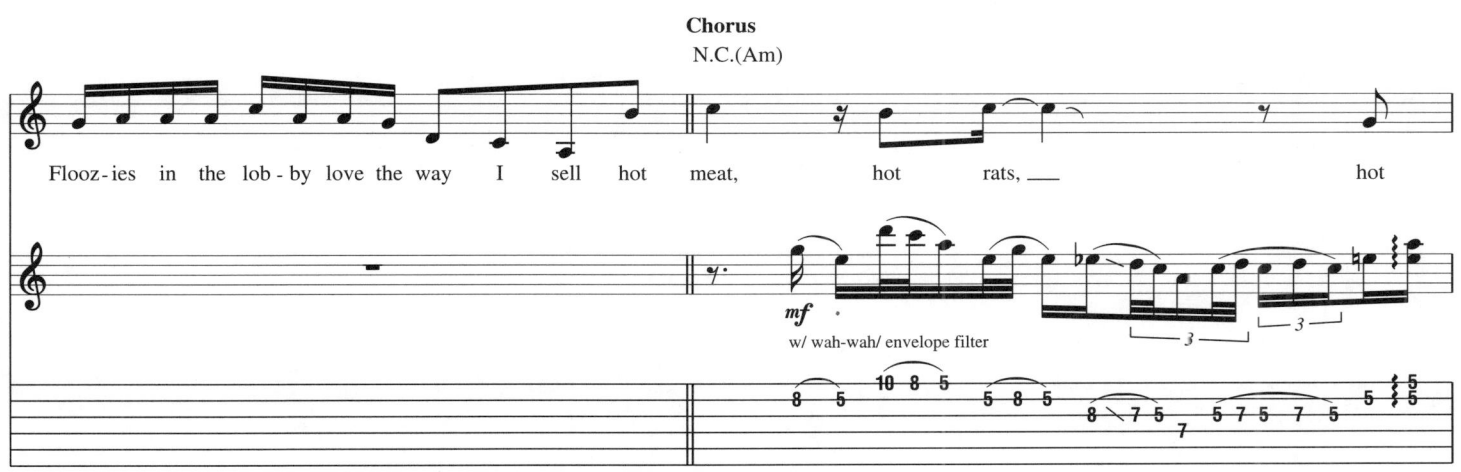

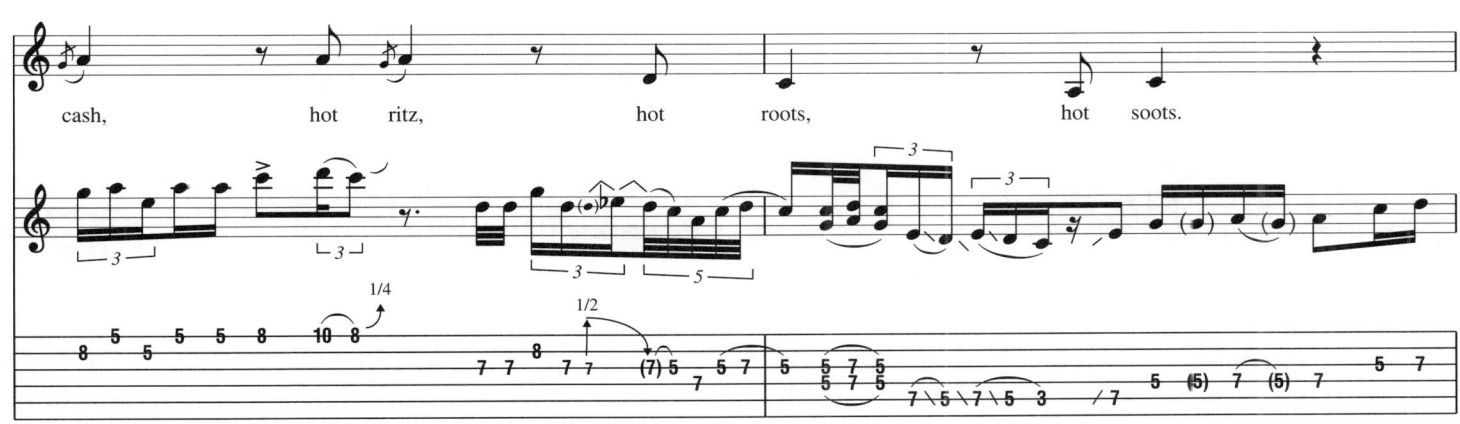

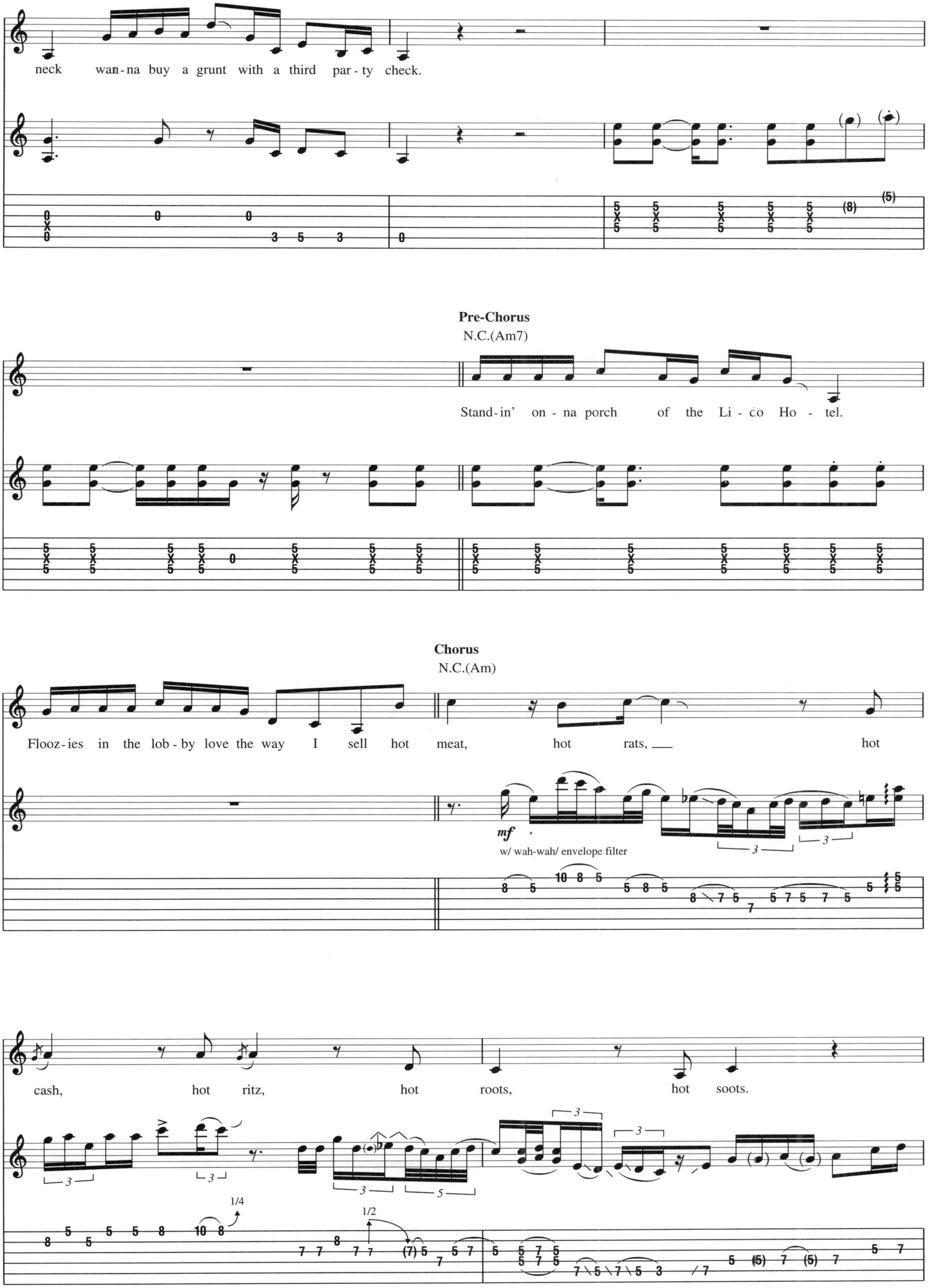

Guitar Solo

N.C.(Am)

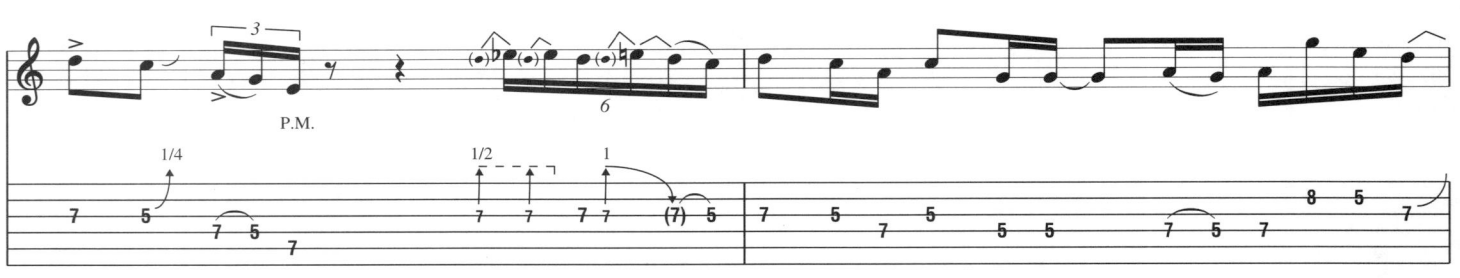

w/ ad-lib. hollering (next 11 meas.)

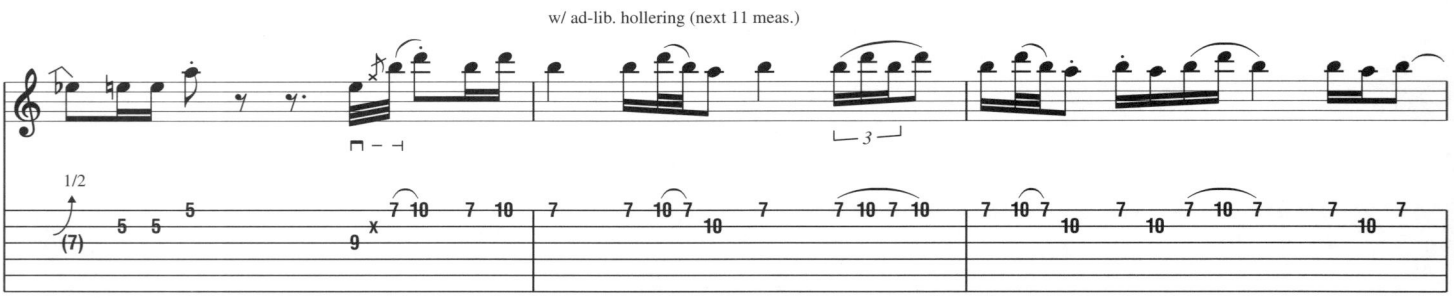

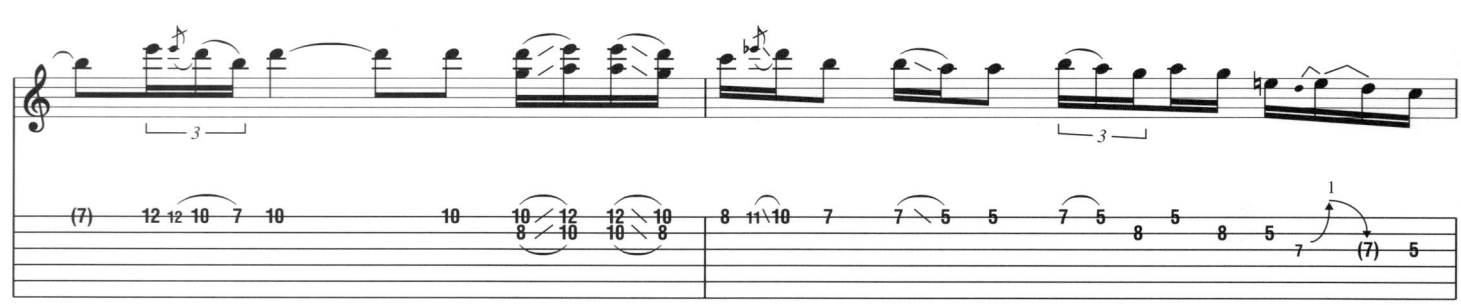

Chorus
N.C.(Am)

Hot, meat, hot rats, hot Jacks, ___ hot zitz, hot roots, hot soots.

Guitar Solo
N.C.(Am)

Oh.

= Played as even sixteenth notes.

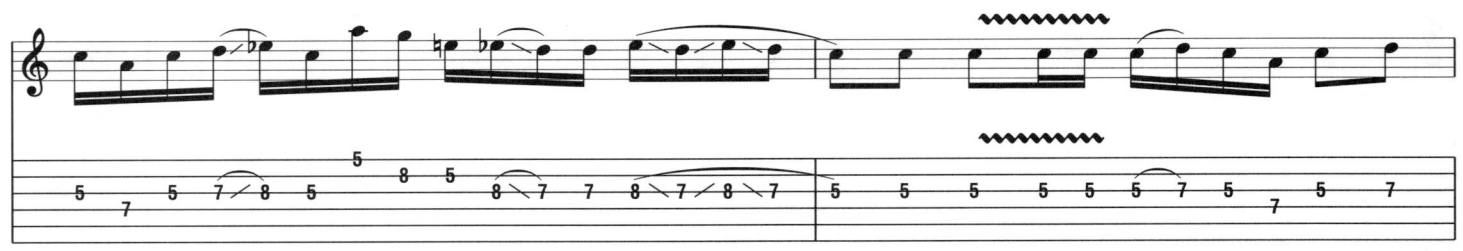

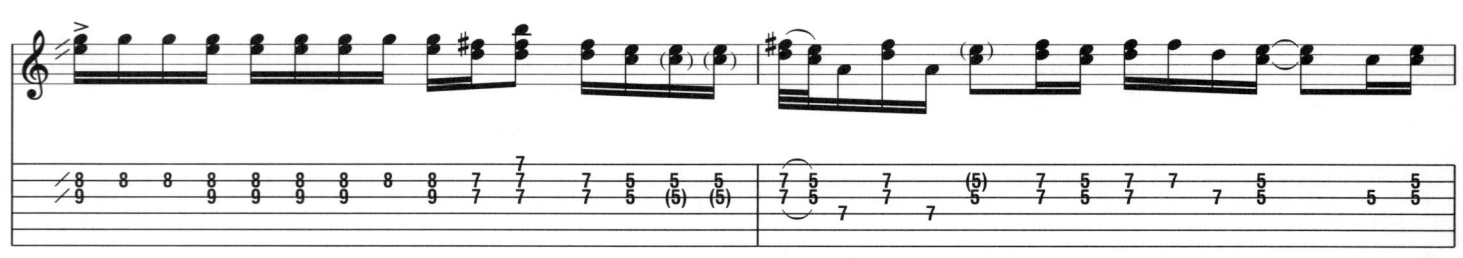
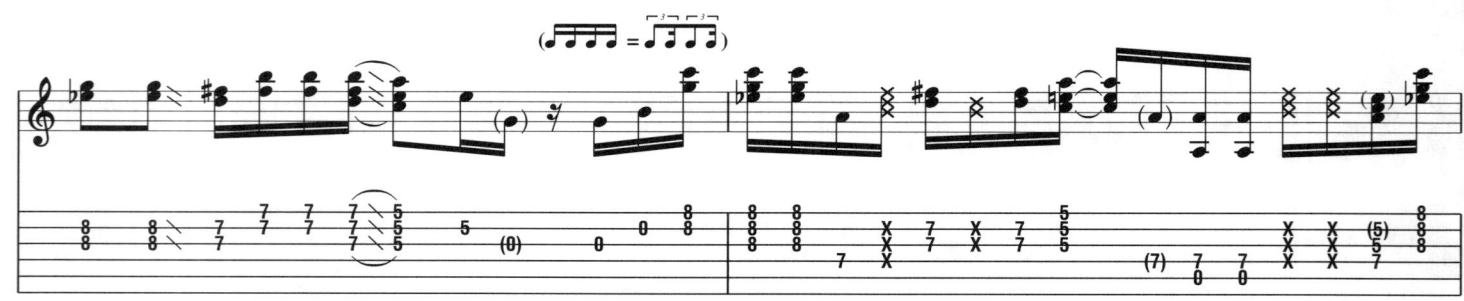

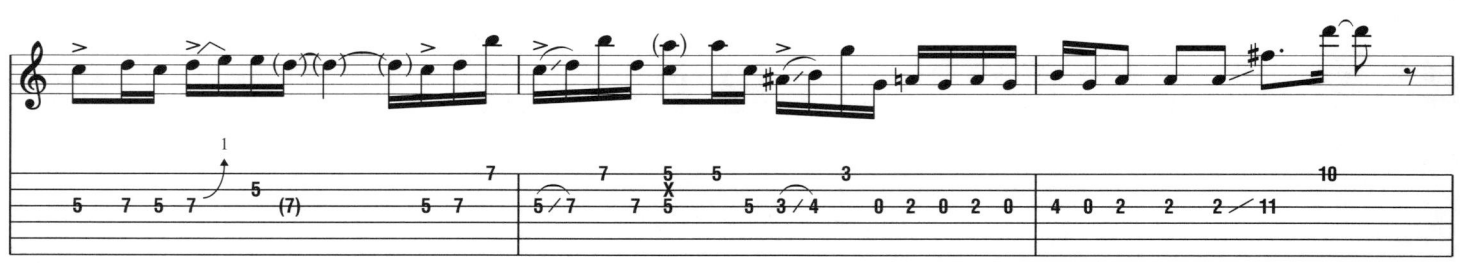

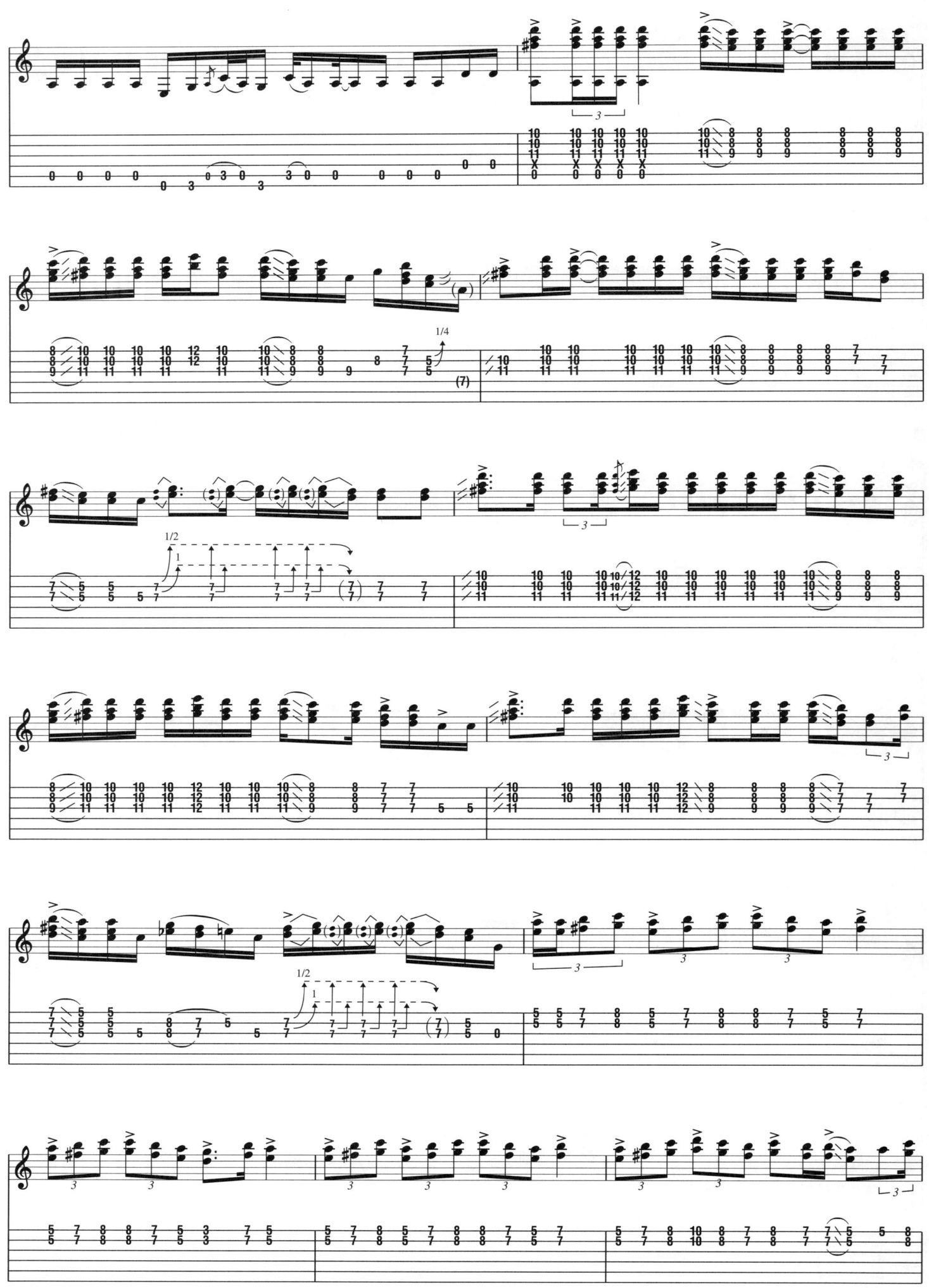

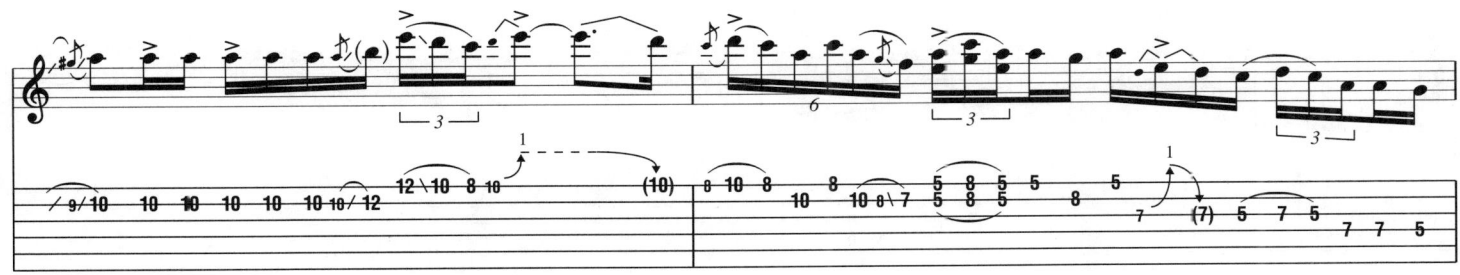

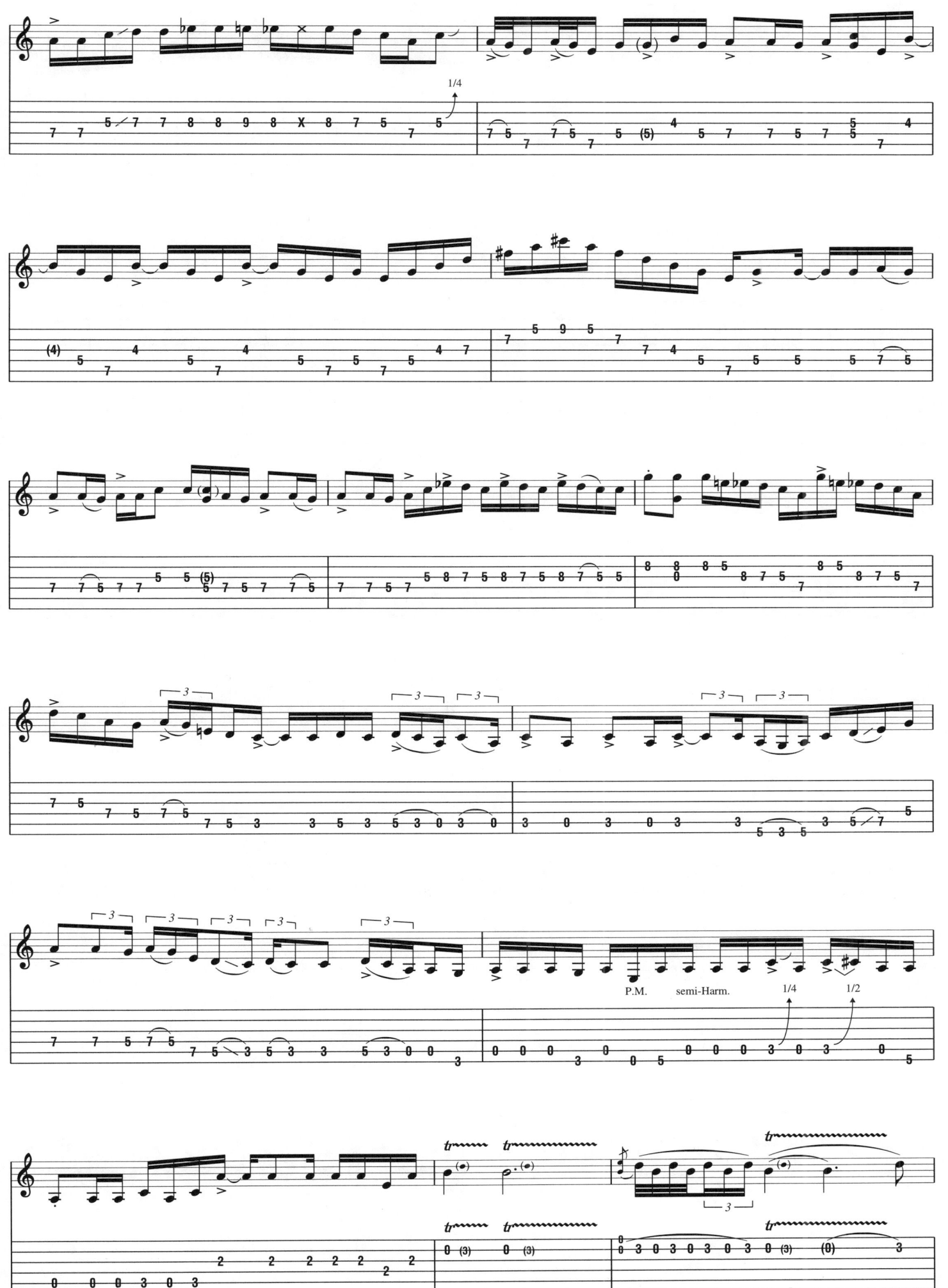

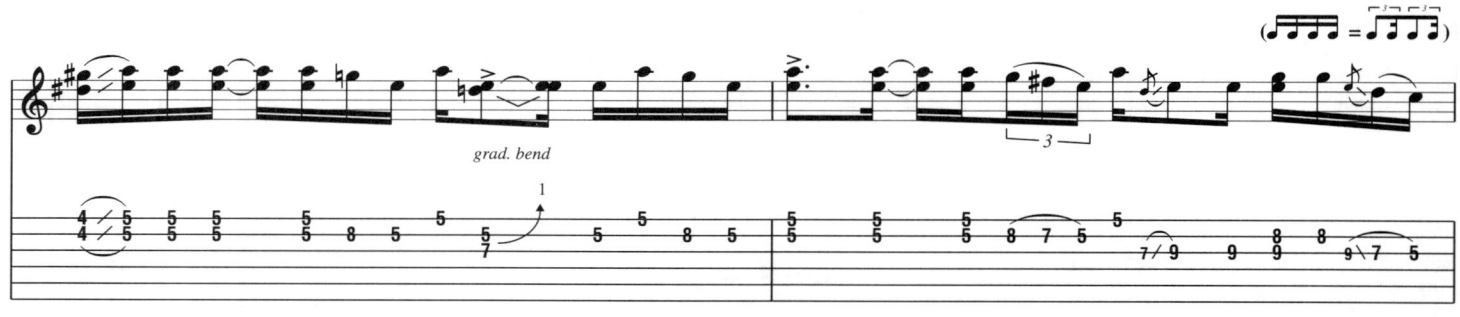

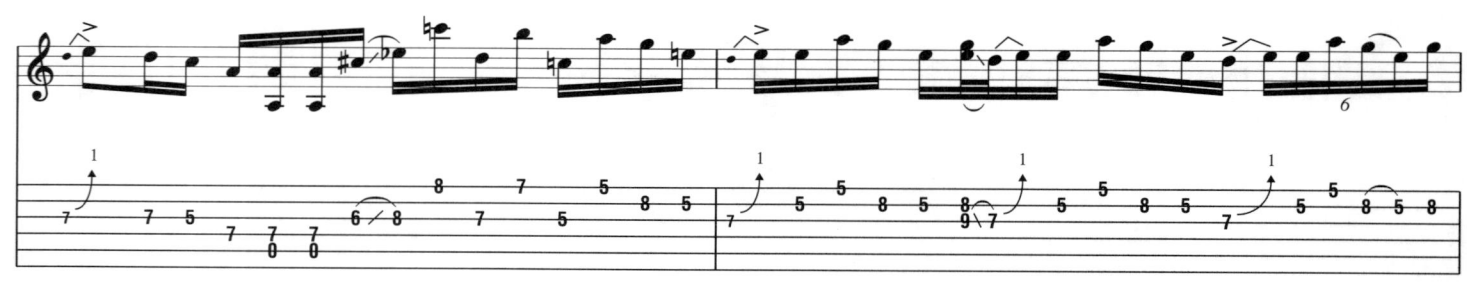

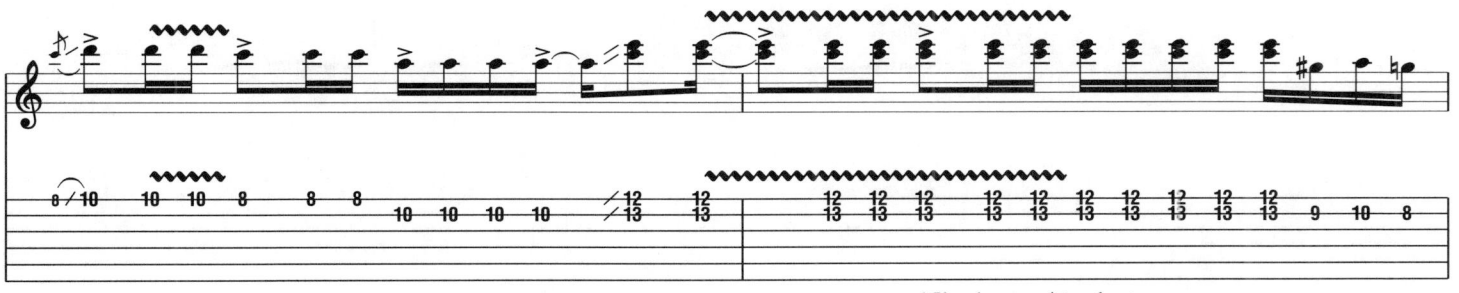

* Played as even sixteenth notes.

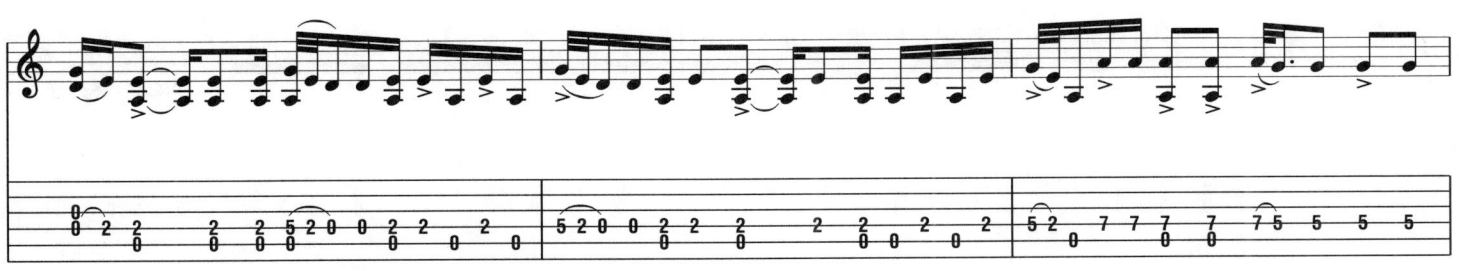

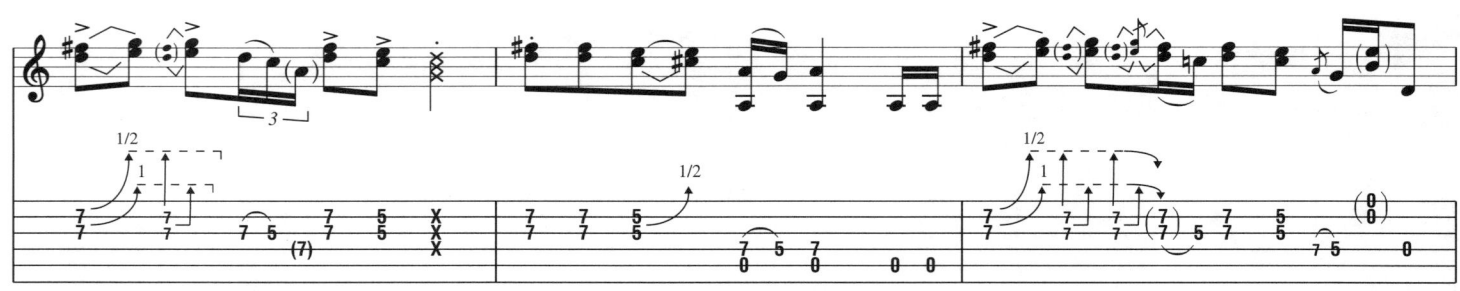

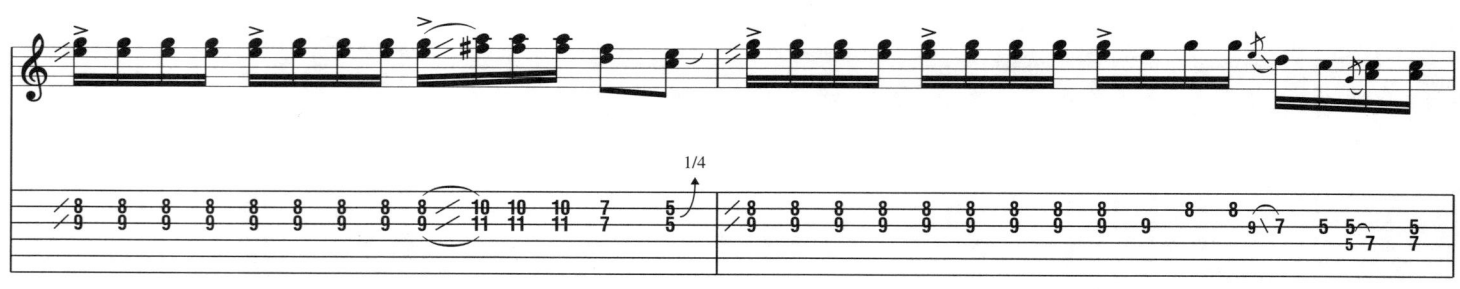

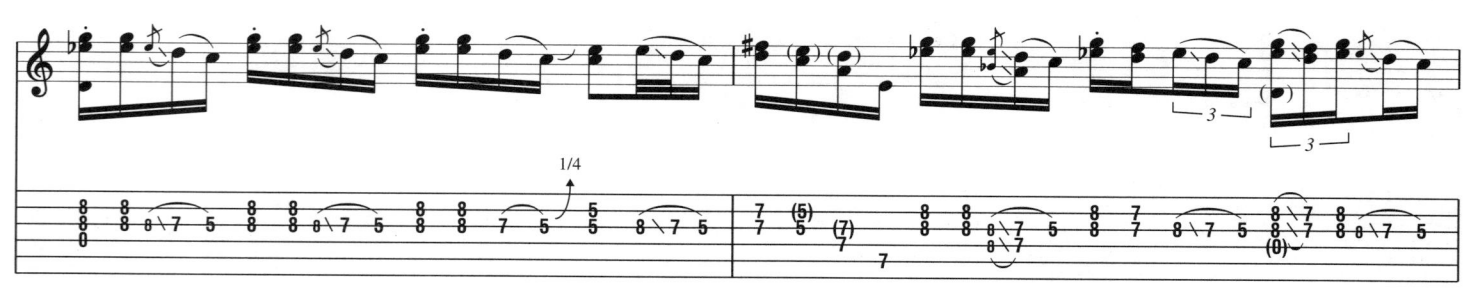

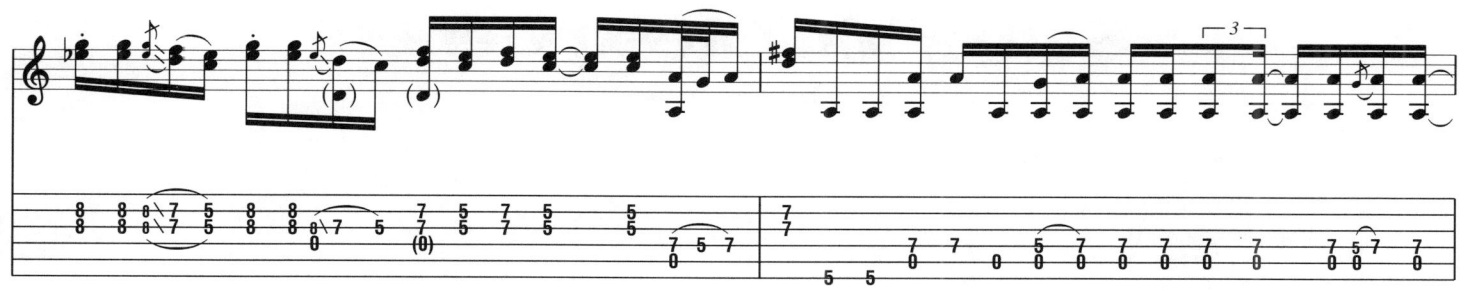

Outro

N.C.(Am)

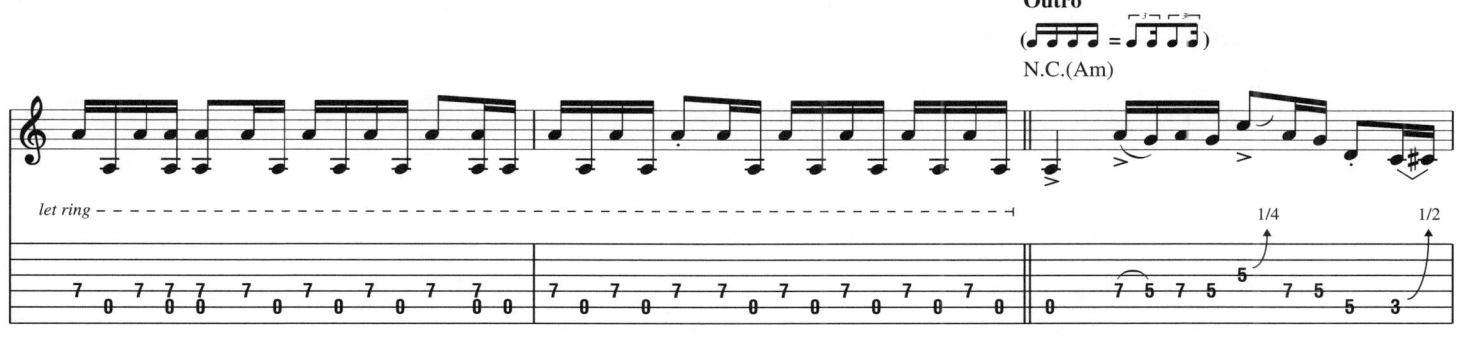

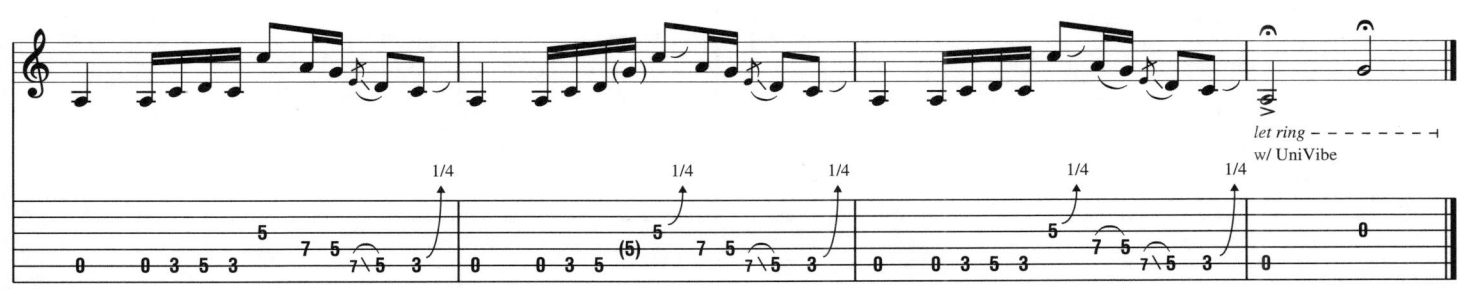

Son of Mr. Green Genes

By Frank Zappa

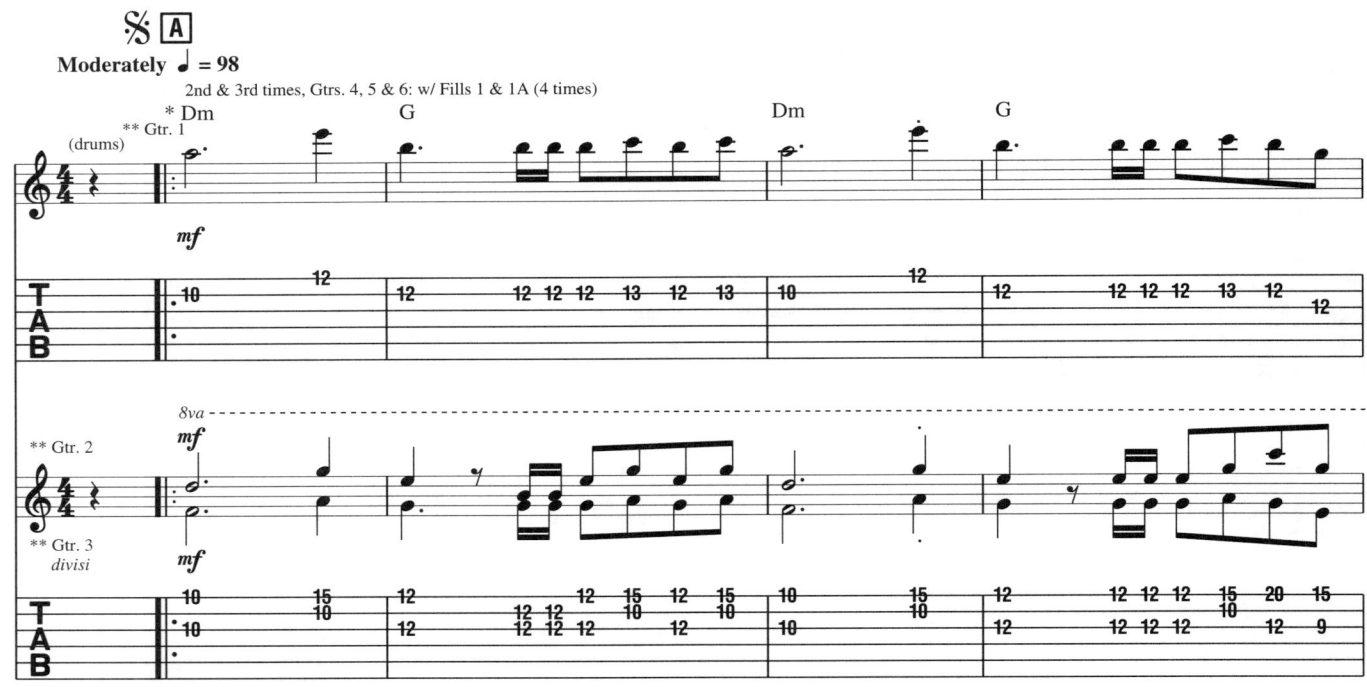

* Chord symbols reflect overall harmony.
** Horns arr. for gtr.

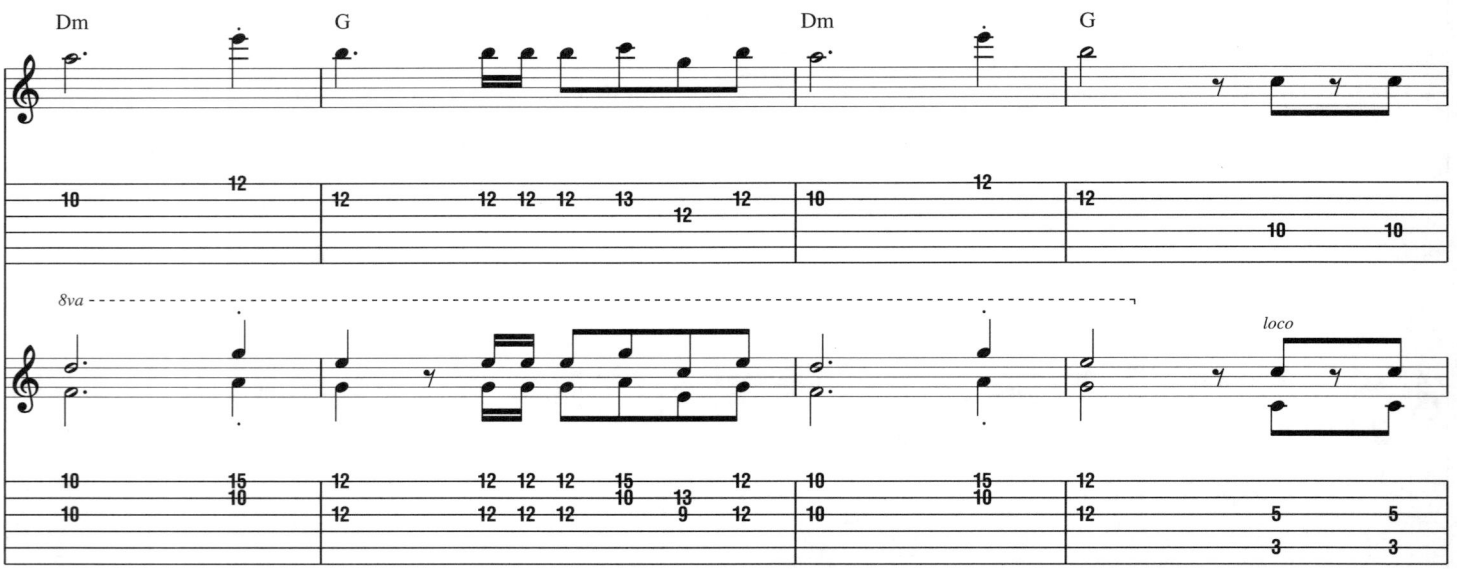

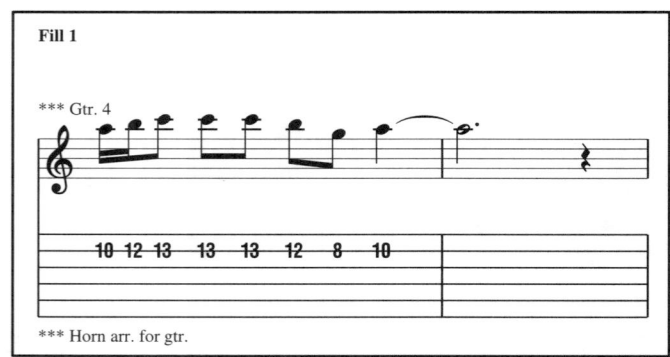

*** Horn arr. for gtr.

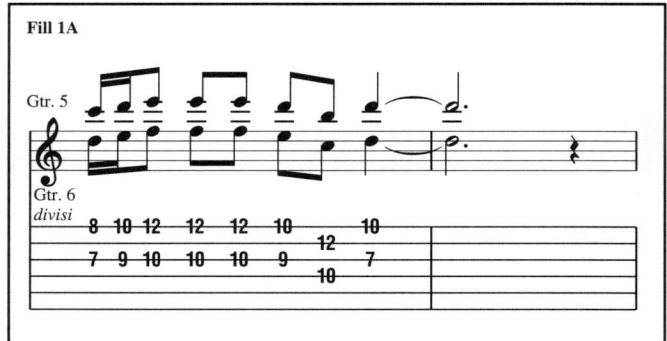

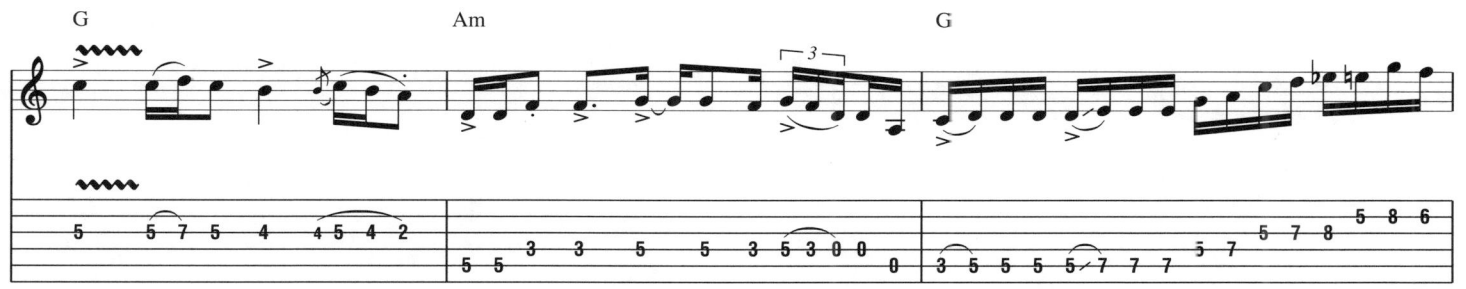
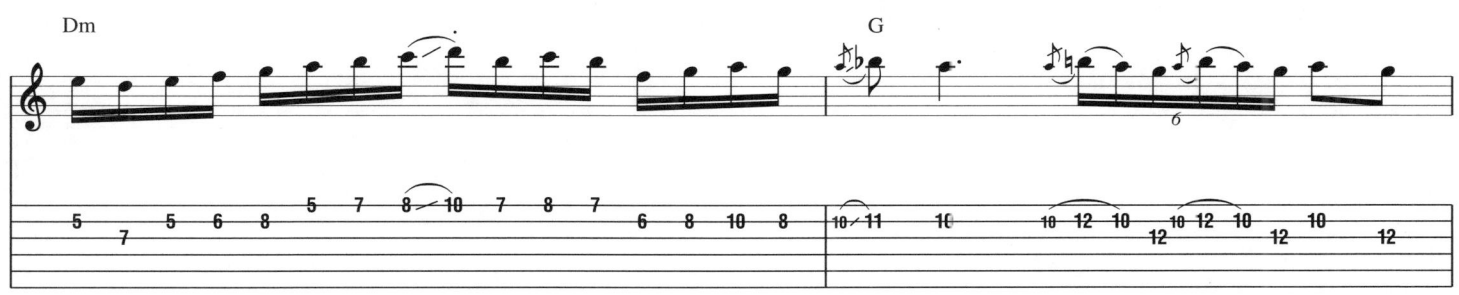

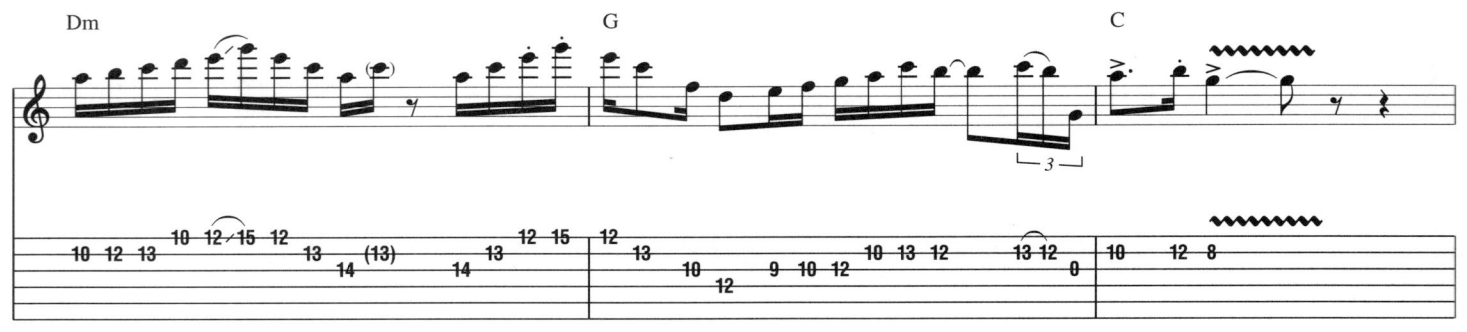
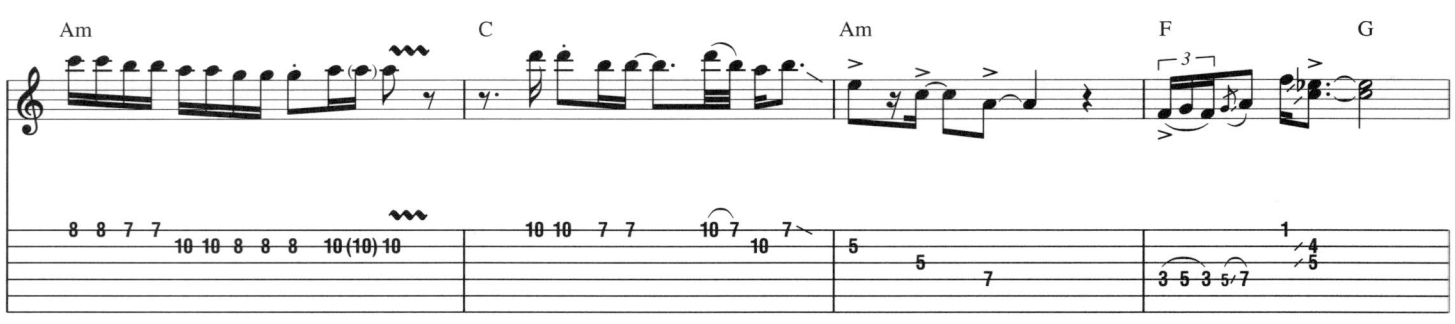
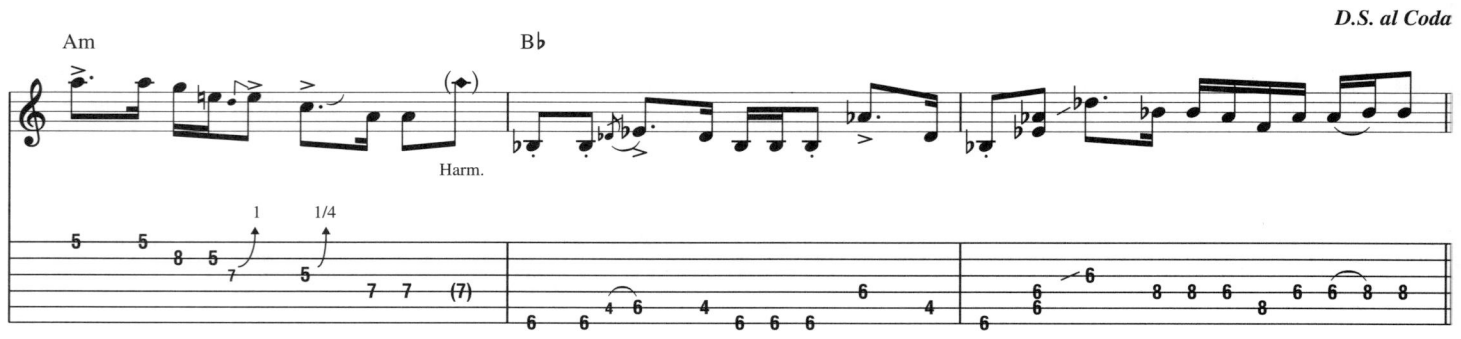
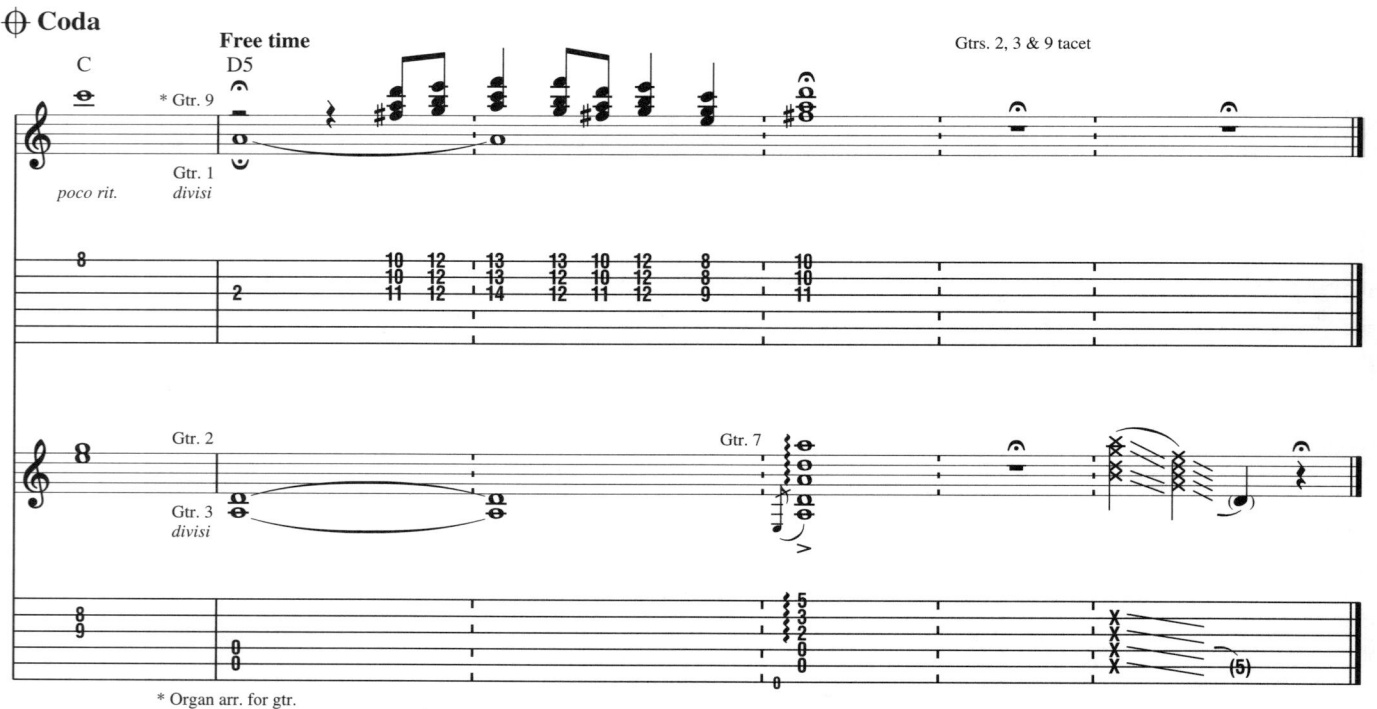

Little Umbrellas

By Frank Zappa

The Gumbo Variations

By Frank Zappa

C Sax Solo

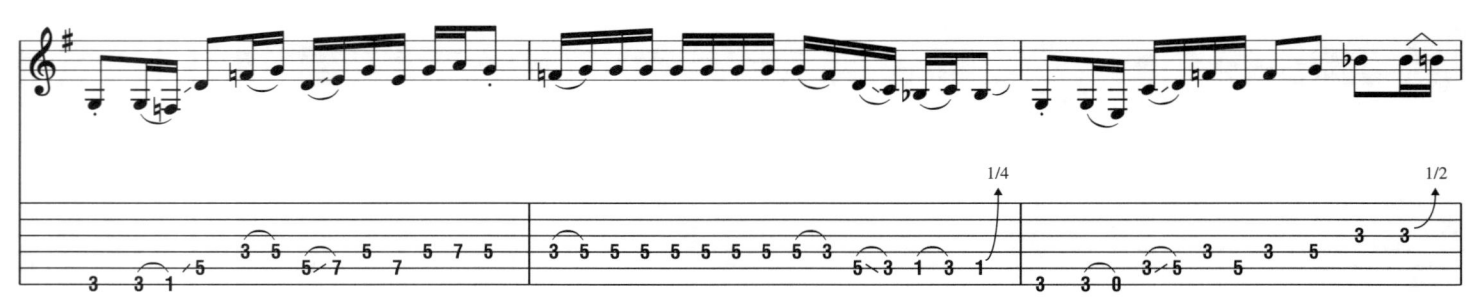

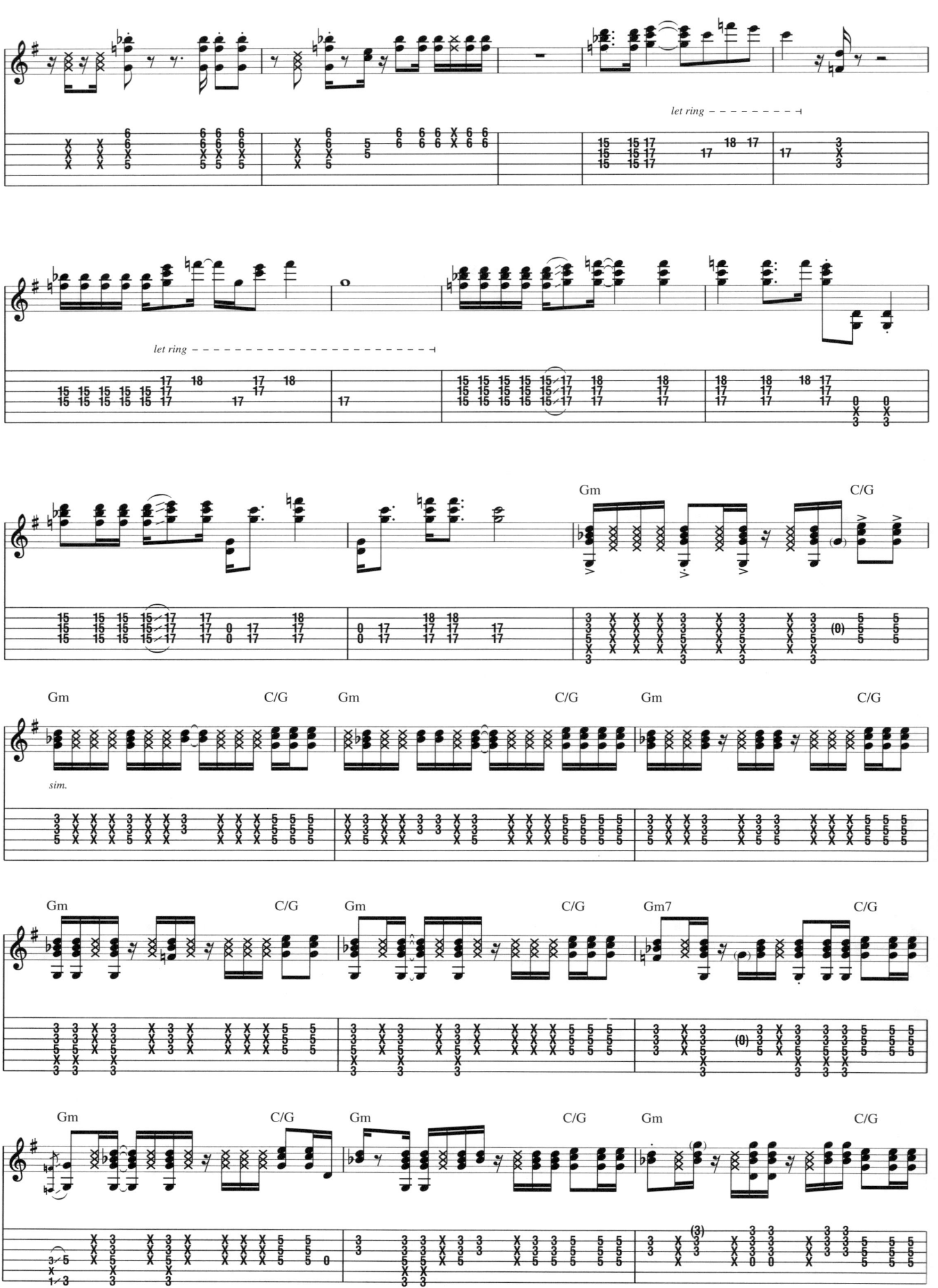

It Must Be a Camel

By Frank Zappa

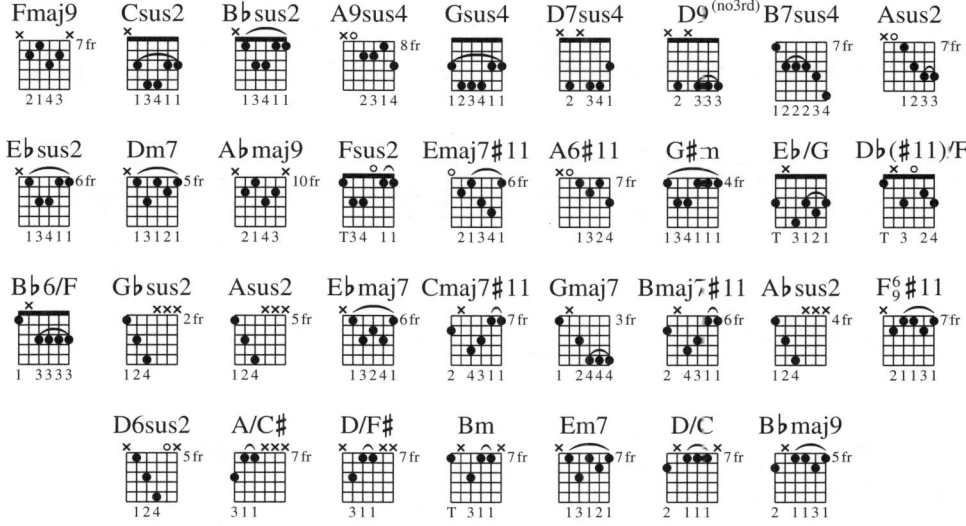

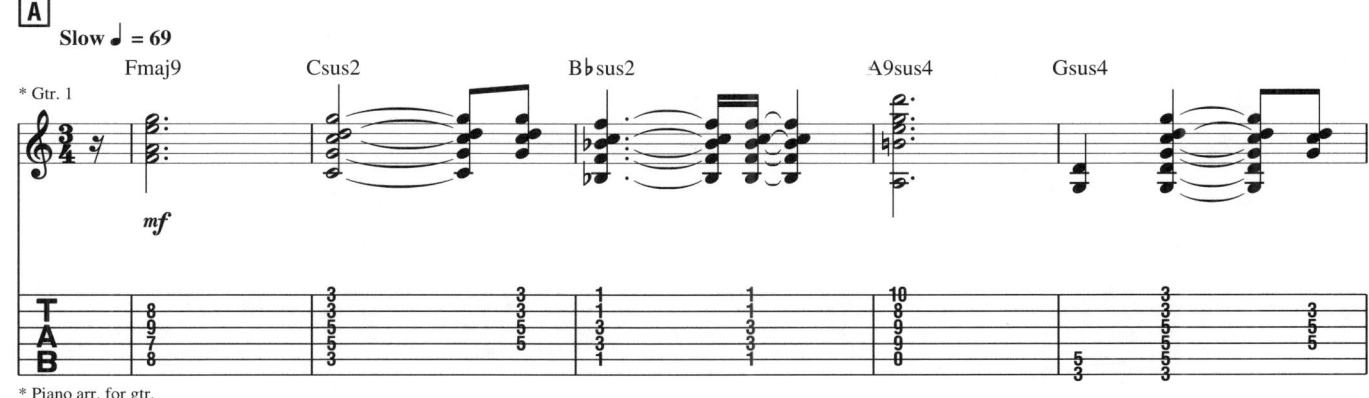

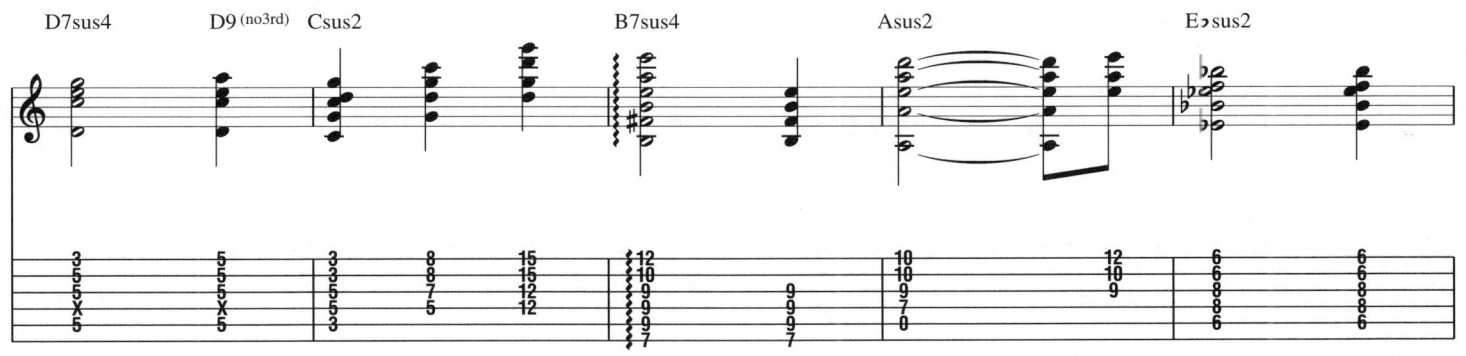

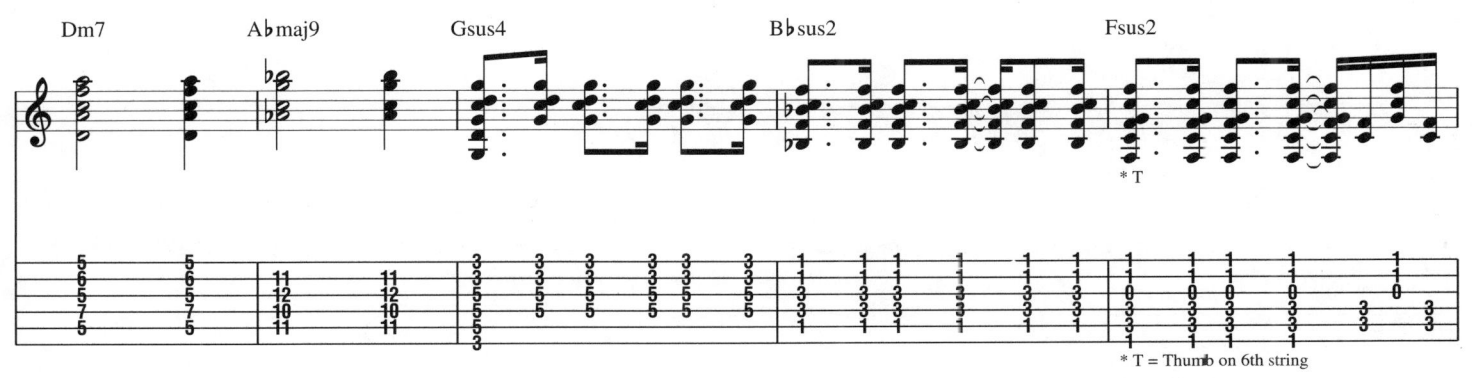

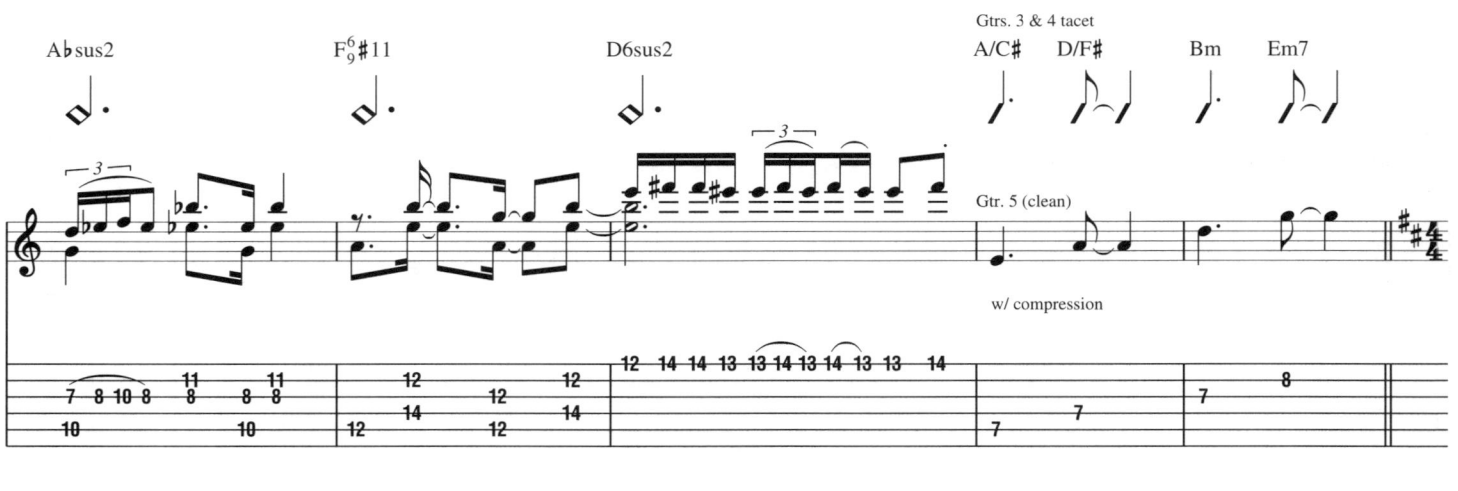
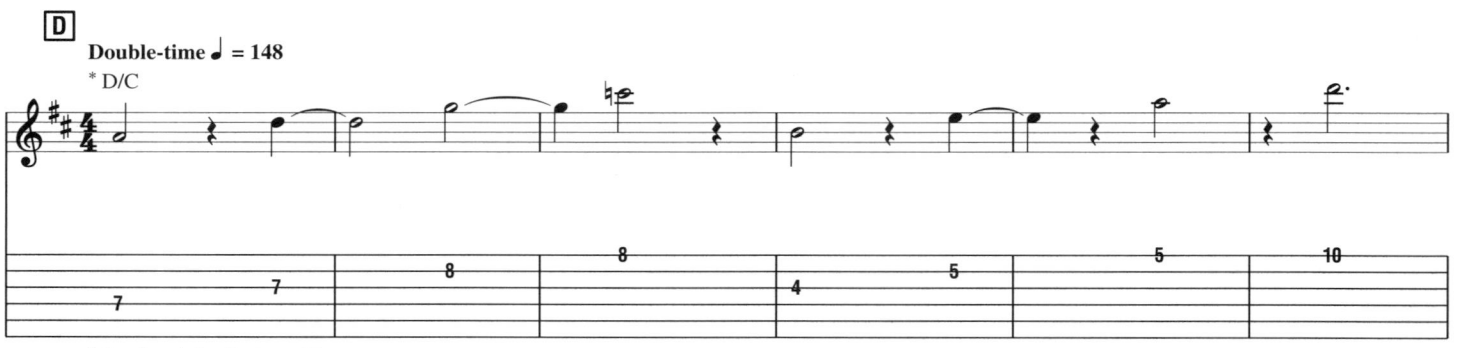
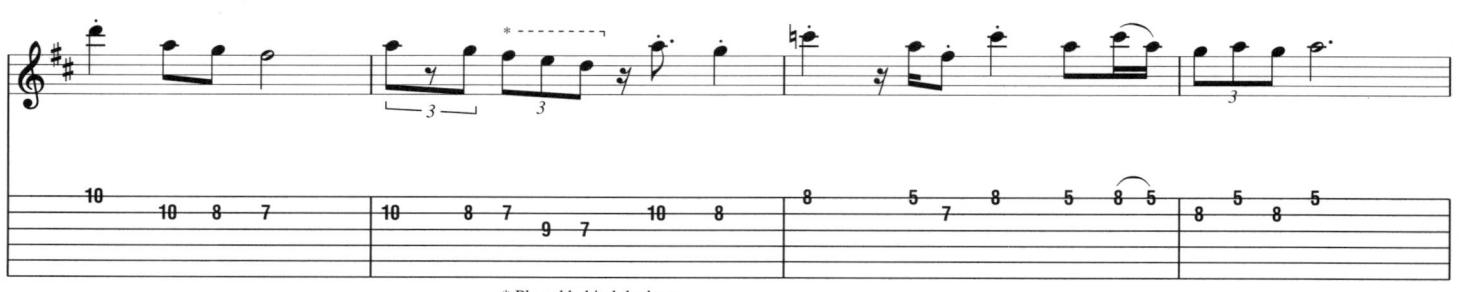
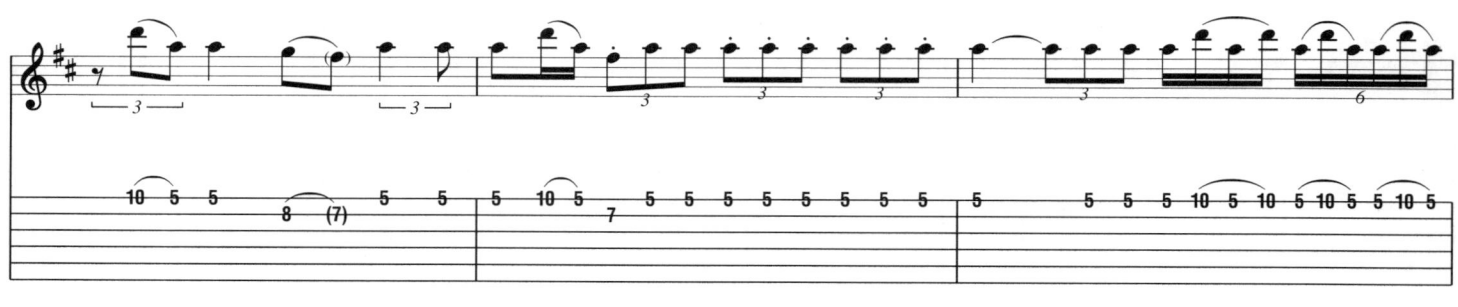
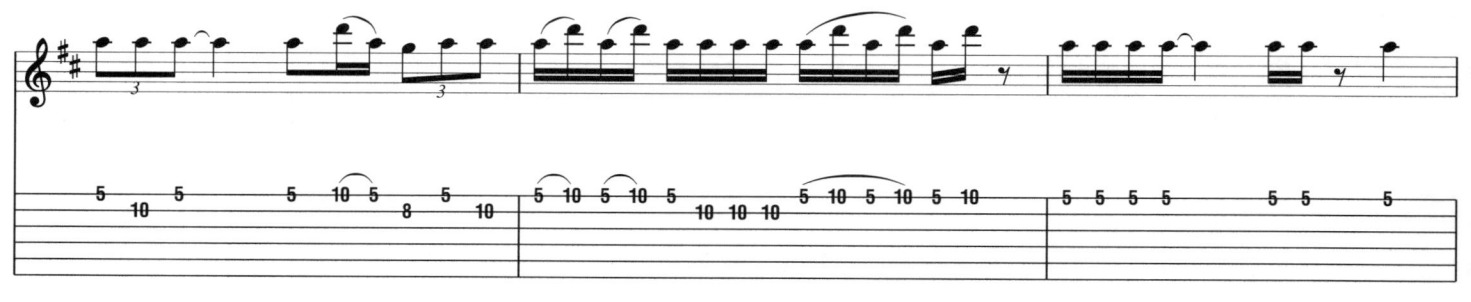

Guitar Notation Legend

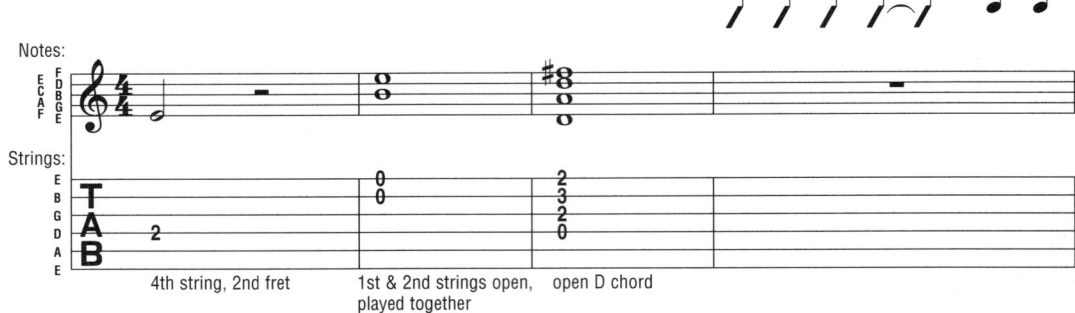

Guitar Music can be notated three different ways: on a *musical staff*, in *tablature*, and in *rhythm slashes*.

RHYTHM SLASHES are written above the staff. Strum chords in the rhythm indicated. Use the chord diagrams found at the top of the first page of the transcription for the appropriate chord voicings. Round noteheads indicate single notes.

THE MUSICAL STAFF shows pitches and rhythms and is divided by bar lines into measures. Pitches are named after the first seven letters of the alphabet.

TABLATURE graphically represents the guitar fingerboard. Each horizontal line represents a string, and each number represents a fret.

HALF-STEP BEND: Strike the note and bend up 1/2 step.

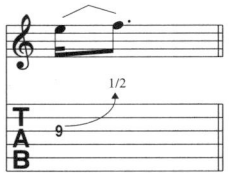

WHOLE-STEP BEND: Strike the note and bend up one step.

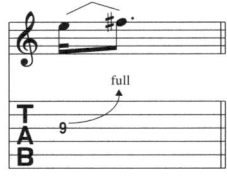

GRACE NOTE BEND: Strike the note and bend up as indicated. The first note does not take up any time.

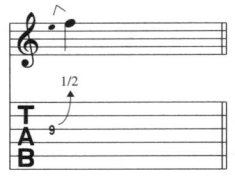

SLIGHT (MICROTONE) BEND: Strike the note and bend up 1/4 step.

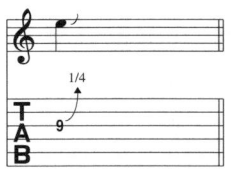

BEND AND RELEASE: Strike the note and bend up as indicated, then release back to the original note. Only the first note is struck.

PRE-BEND: Bend the note as indicated, then strike it.

VIBRATO: The string is vibrated by rapidly bending and releasing the note with the fretting hand.

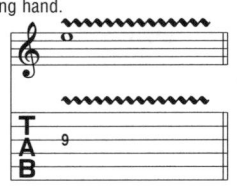

WIDE VIBRATO: The pitch is varied to a greater degree by vibrating with the fretting hand.

HAMMER-ON: Strike the first (lower) note with one finger, then sound the higher note (on the same string) with another finger by fretting it without picking.

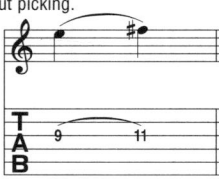

PULL-OFF: Place both fingers on the notes to be sounded. Strike the first note and without picking, pull the finger off to sound the second (lower) note.

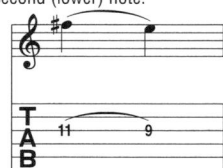

LEGATO SLIDE: Strike the first note and then slide the same fret-hand finger up or down to the second note. The second note is not struck.

SHIFT SLIDE: Same as legato slide, except the second note is struck.

TRILL: Very rapidly alternate between the notes indicated by continuously hammering on and pulling off.

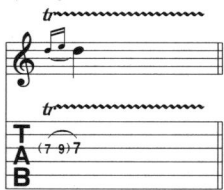

TAPPING: Hammer ("tap") the fret indicated with the pick-hand index or middle finger and pull off to the note fretted by the fret hand.

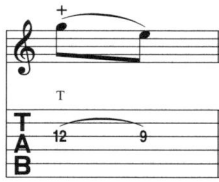

NATURAL HARMONIC: Strike the note while the fret-hand lightly touches the string directly over the fret indicated.

PINCH HARMONIC: The note is fretted normally and a harmonic is produced by adding the edge of the thumb or the tip of the index finger of the pick hand to the normal pick attack.

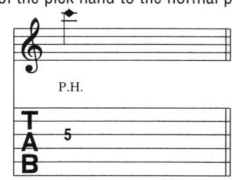

PICK SCRAPE: The edge of the pick is rubbed down (or up) the string, producing a scratchy sound.

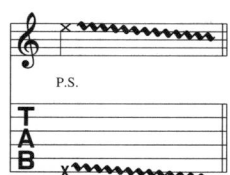

MUFFLED STRINGS: A percussive sound is produced by laying the fret hand across the string(s) without depressing, and striking them with the pick hand.

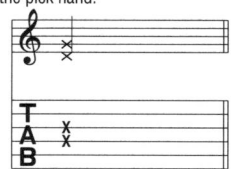

PALM MUTING: The note is partially muted by the pick hand lightly touching the string(s) just before the bridge.

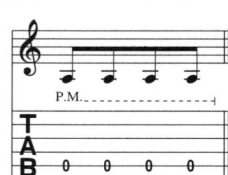

RAKE: Drag the pick across the strings indicated with a single motion.

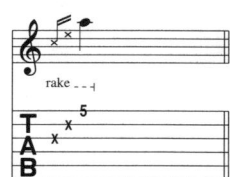

TREMOLO PICKING: The note is picked as rapidly and continuously as possible.

VIBRATO BAR DIVE AND RETURN: The pitch of the note or chord is dropped a specified number of steps (in rhythm) then returned to the original pitch.

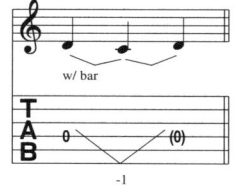

VIBRATO BAR SCOOP: Depress the bar just before striking the note, then quickly release the bar.

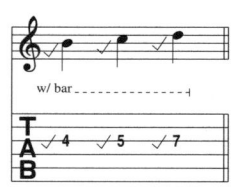

VIBRATO BAR DIP: Strike the note and then immediately drop a specified number of steps, then release back to the original pitch.